You're Special

D1520613

KATHERINE THOMAS LEURCK

You're Special

DAILY REFLECTIONS FROM GOD'S CHILDREN WITH "EXCEPTIONALITIES"

outskirts
press

To Dave, my love and my life

To my children, Andrew, Alexandra, and Audrey,
who are all my inspiration

To my family, and especially my parents,
who taught me that love sees all exceptionalities

To the Leurck family, who shower me with love
and view each child as a ray of God's sunshine

To my sister Denise and my Posse, who have loved
and supported me on this journey and in life

To all of God's children, as you are
the light of God's love on this earth!

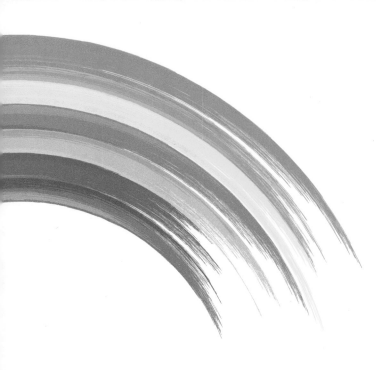

A portion of the proceeds of this book will support Drew's Rainbow Foundation, an organization that supports individuals with exceptionalities and recognizes the "special" in everyone.

Dear Readers,

The beauty and curse of our son Drew's interpretation of the world is that he views it quite literally. This is good because he is not bogged down by the minutiae of life and simply takes things at face value. While this presents an obvious risk, his perspective also holds much truth.

Drew views the world through the eyes of an innocent child—eyes that have not been clouded. He is not burdened by societal acceptance, standards, or concern with future success. His chronological age is twenty-three, but his "exceptionalities" have kept him cognitively at age seven. Where my eyes are often clouded, Drew's lens is very clear.

His clarity has taught me so much. His literal interpretations have shed light on my perspective and outlook on the world, which has brought so much joy. I hope they also provide insight and joy to the reader.

Love, hugs, and rainbows,

Drew's mom

Katherine Thomas Leurck

Cover Art

The artwork on the cover of *You're Special* is an original painting by my husband, Dave Leurck. He captures the beauty of our son and how Drew always sees the light. Drew looks up with hope and love, which has led him to his rainbows.

In the foreground, you will notice pieces of paper embedded in the painting. These are actual shredded reports from "experts" with dismal and grim predictions for Drew's future.

We elected to see Drew and his future differently. We elected to see what he could do, what he could say, what he could teach, whom he could inspire.

We elected to see the "special" in Drew.

Preface:

The journey of understanding, accepting,
and celebrating our son with exceptionalities.

UNDERSTANDING

Many of the Rainbow Reflections shared in this book are all about celebrating the beauty of Drew, and also his peers--but this journey has not always been that easy.

What I am about to write might be a bit shocking, but honest. Drew was possibly the most perfect gift we never wished for. That is very different from never wanted or loved, simply never wished for.

Most newly expectant parents don't raise their hand and say, "Pick me, pick me!" when God is passing out the children with exceptionalities. Although, knowing what we know now, they should!

Generally, it is quite the opposite. At the first ultrasound it is common to nervously ask, "Is everything okay," and "Does the baby look healthy?"

With pregnancy, dreams begin. This is normal and how it should be, as one of the biggest signs of hope in this challenging world is a newborn baby.

Drew, the first of our three wonderful children, is born August 28, 1998—precious, healthy, and with a good set of lungs! He hits his milestones and sits up, crawls, and walks on time; however, he is quiet. Drew does not do a lot of babbling or cooing, and first words come late and slow.

At age two, Drew still isn't talking, and we are told Drew is severely apraxic, which is the first of many diagnoses.

We "UNDERSTAND" there is an issue, but we are determined to fix him. We consume much of our life, time, energy, and finances chasing hope.

The school recommends further testing, and a team of experts evaluate Drew. Still not accepting any of the diagnosis or labels we've been given, we welcome the evaluation and cannot wait for these experts to see that Drew is just fine.

A week after testing, I get a call that the results are in and the team would like me to come to the office on Monday to review. They must be crazy; how am I supposed to wait over a weekend? I request that they tell me the results on the phone, as I'm confident that it is good news.

After much pleading, the psychologist finally concedes and explains that Andrew is cognitively delayed.

Unsure what the term "cognitively delayed" implies, I ask if this is connected with ADHD, dyslexia, autism? I share my confusion and the psychologist is silent.

I fear the silence.

After what seems like forever, she says, "Mrs. Leurck, they used to refer to cognitive delay as mental retardation, but the term cognitive delay is how we now refer to Drew's diagnosis."

I drop the phone.

ACCEPTING

Accepting happens slowly and not fully until Drew is about ten years old. It takes many "punch in the gut" moments to finally ACCEPT.

One poignant moment occurs in kindergarten. Our family is so excited to attend Drew's first open house. We go into his classroom where there is a bulletin board of student artwork.

We scan the board excitedly looking for Drew's drawing. There are many wonderful and creative drawings of houses, pets, families, and self-portraits.

My eyes finally settle on a drawing that is completely discombobulated. It is a detached self-portrait with eyes drawn on one part of the page and legs elsewhere. Then I see the name, which is spelled incorrectly and backwards, and I realize this is Drew's work.

I immediately go up to the teacher and ask, "Why did you include 1st and 2nd graders' artwork on this board?"

She looks me in the eye and confirms, "This is all kindergarten work; this is the work of Drew and his peers."

The disparity is so obvious that I struggle to hide my heartbreak as I quickly make my exit.

Over the years there are many more "punch in the gut" moments, and each with a new wave of grief. I begin to question, "What if this can't be fixed?"

Time passes and boys become young men; they get their driver's license and take girls to dances while Drew and I still play matchbox cars on the kitchen floor.

I begin to accept.

Accepting is very different from giving up. Accepting is to appreciate Drew for who he is and to maximize his potential.

I accept that in Pee Wee football, the highlight of the game and the only time Drew is on the field is when they announce, "No. 4 Andrew Leurck."

I accept, that at swim meets, when the other lanes have finished the race, Andrew still has two laps to go.

I accept that at eighteen, Drew still jumps up and down like a five-year-old when he sees Santa at Macy's.

CELEBRATING

This brings us to the BEST part of the journey: celebrating Drew!

When we stop trying to fix Drew, or change Drew, or improve Drew, we see Drew.

He is beautiful and he is perfect just as he is; there is nothing to fix, and he is a light of God's love on this earth. We realize that he is a connector and a teacher and that he inspires.

Drew has taught us that we are all exactly how we are intended to be. God is in each of us, and we are here to learn from one another.

Drew teaches us that we all have beautiful gifts. You might have an important title, you might have a degree, or you might just say "I love you" every day.

Some of us die and we never get it; some of us get it right before we die. Drew gets it, and he has from day one. He is a simple boy on this earth with a very simple message – just love and be loving!

As it turns out, Drew is the best gift we never wished for but one of the greatest gifts we ever got!

Always Remember "You're Special"

This daily devotional may seem quite different from others, and that's because it is. It is inspired by the words and actions of individuals with exceptionalities.

The voices heard from the pages of this book include children with autism, Down syndrome, Williams syndrome, and cognition delay, to name a few. The language is simple, pure, and reflects my experience with this remarkable community, which I consider to be angels among us.

This book is one of the first of its kind because it provides children with exceptionalities a limitless platform to teach and inspire. While often this community is encouraged to "change" or "improve," these individuals, in my experience, are quite perfect just as they are, and we can learn so much from them.

Have you ever seen a person wheelchair bound with a smile on his face that was bigger than you've smiled all week? Or a child with Down syndrome who is in a perpetual good mood and wonder, *What's the magic?*

Chances are when you interact with these people, you will walk away in awe of their grounded trust in themselves and others, free of expectations. You will likely have a better day as a result of the interaction.

I am the mother of three wonderful children and one of them, Drew, just happens to be cognitively delayed. At least once a day, I am inspired, reminded, or flat out confronted with love from the distinct voice and perspective of my child.

How could I keep this to myself?

Let's be eager students of individuals with exceptionalities and their unique experience. They have so much to share, and we have so much to gain! It's where "special" meets truth—and in truth, there is wisdom.

Enjoy your 365 days of reflections and embrace Drew's purposeful words: "You're Special."

JANUARY 1

Rainbow Reflection: Remember That Love Is the Answer

Drew's diagnosis has been a realization that hasn't always been easy. In fact, it has been quite an emotional journey. When Drew was about seven, he began making me a rainbow every day. Some days one, other days ten, but rarely a day goes by that he doesn't put his hands behind his back and say, "Mommy, I have something for you!" Of course, I act surprised and say, "I can't imagine what it could be?" He generally shouts, "It's your rainbow!" while grinning ear to ear.

After Drew had been doing this for a year, we were on a bike trail and I asked him, "Why do you make me these rainbows every day?" He looked at me as if I were ignorant and said, "Mommy, a rainbow is a sign of God's love!"

He was right, as I recalled the story of Noah's Ark. After the earth was flooded, Noah came out of the ark to find beautiful rainbows, which were a covenant of hope and everlasting love. But I had never shared this story with Drew.

The following night I tucked Drew in bed and asked, "Hey buddy, how did you know about the rainbow being a sign of God's love? Did you read it in a book? Did Grandma tell you?"

Drew replied, "Nope, but sometimes when I sleep at night, I sit on Jesus's lap, and he told me!"

I was speechless, but the rainbows have been coming ever since. Stacks, piles, and bins of them! I just can't throw them away. He generally dates them and often writes a message such as "I like your food," or "I love you to Jesus and back," and "You're Special," which is so poignant coming from Drew. He has given them to family,

1

friends, and anyone who stops in our home, which has included the handyman, who replied, "Uh, thanks, little dude. I'm keeping this in my truck!"

They are on refrigerators, wallets, dashboards, dorms, businesses, and offices across America. His rainbows have even gone global. Drew passed them out in Spain, Italy, France, England, and Mexico, and his message translates beautifully. Strangers, many of whom do not speak English, are so receptive, often giving him a hug or at minimum a big smile! To date, Drew has passed out over 20,0000 rainbow cards.

On September 10, 2016, we honored Drew and his beautiful rainbows by gift wrapping our home with them.

We utilized over 3000 of his hand-drawn rainbows to wrap the entire outside of our home. The goal was to make our home his canvas to showcase his beautiful rainbow art and message of love.

"The House that Andrew Built." It's all about love!

SCRIPTURE SUPPORT: JOHN 13:34 ESV

A new commandment I give to you, that you love one another:
just as I have loved you, you also are to love one another.

Rainbow Reflection: Remember That God Made Each and Every One of Us Special

Drew is often labeled "special," which confuses him, as he often says, "Mommy, I think that everyone is special."

One day that was not going particularly well, Drew walked into the kitchen to cheer me up with a drawing that said "You're Special." The beauty of him reminding me that I was special, was quite impactful.

This rainbow message is an all-time favorite that continues to be shared around the world.

"You're Special"

SCRIPTURE SUPPORT: SONG OF SOLOMON 4:7 ESV

You are altogether beautiful; my love; there is no flaw in you.

Rainbow Reflection:
Find Peace in Acceptance

From age two, Drew was in therapy. Speech therapy, occupational therapy, cognition therapy, neurological therapy, music therapy, play therapy, and more. Our weeks were filled with doctor appointments.

In the early years and in my mind as a mother, the goal was to "fix" Drew to enable him to be "typical." That all seems so funny now that I have come to realize that he is perfect just how he is made. But on my journey, I wanted Drew to keep up with his peers and to hit all the established milestones.

Years and years, we spent chasing this futile dream, only to realize there was no catching up. In fact, as time passes, the deficits widen and are more apparent. As the classmates progress, so does the gap between my sweet boy and his "typical" friends.

I want to yell, scream, kick, cry, scrape, scratch, and fight for each baby step, but time and evidence beat me down. I yearn for just one report, doctor, or teacher to shout, "Great job, Team Drew; you have made significant progress!" But those words are never spoken. I feel like I'm in a vat and while the sky is opening for all of Drew's peers, we are descending, down, down further from the light.

Then I see him. I look closer and I see him. I see my sweet boy. I see his smile. I see his rainbows. I see his love. I see his light.

As I watch him sleep, I kiss his head through my streaming tears and quietly pray for his and God's forgiveness, for Drew is perfect, just how he is.

All these years it has been more about what I wanted. I want him to be typical, I want him to make the grades, I want him to play sports, etc. But all along he is smiling his big happy smile, content to be Drew.

I FINALLY see him and let it be.

SCRIPTURE SUPPORT: JOHN 14:27

Peace I leave with you; my peace I give to you. Not as the world gives do, I give to you. Let not your hearts be troubled, neither let them be afraid.

Rainbow Reflection:
See Beauty in the Less Obvious

"Look at all my beautiful shells!"

On beach vacations, Drew will spend hours shelling. He fills bucket after bucket with shells. He sits in awe and amazement at the beauty of every shell he collects. At the end of the day, he proudly shows our family his collection. We scratch our heads, so confused about why he would pick up most of these shells. Almost all are cracked, broken, and faded. Few, if any, of his shells are in perfect condition. Drew, however, sees each one as unique and beautiful in their own special way, and he cherishes his collection. Interestingly, Drew looks at his shells the way God must look at us. He looks beyond the cracks, broken pieces, and faded colors. Drew sees the beauty in all, yet Drew is labeled "significantly delayed." If only the world could be so "delayed."

SCRIPTURE SUPPORT: EPHESIANS 4:18 ESV

They are darkened in their understanding, alienated from the life of God because of the ignorance that is in them, due to their hardness of heart.

Rainbow Reflection:
See God's Beauty in All Creation

"Everything is important to God and I see God in flowers, in people, and even in Fiona at the Cincinnati zoo. I see God in everything!"

SCRIPTURE SUPPORT: LUKE 12:6 ESV

Are not five sparrows sold for two pennies?
And not one of them is forgotten before God.

Rainbow Reflection:
See God in Others

Drew struggles to walk past homeless individuals and he has such heartbreak regarding people with no home. At times during dinner prayer or at church, he will randomly start crying and say, "It is not fair that some people don't have a home."

On a visit to New York City, Drew was compelled to interact with every homeless person he saw. Upon seeing one man, Drew stopped, knelt, and gave him a very long hug. The homeless man did not let go and the embrace lasted for quite some time. Before Drew walked away, he gave the homeless man a rainbow card. Upon reading "You're Special," the man said, "Thank you; I needed that. God bless you, Drew."

SCRIPTURE SUPPORT 1 JOHN 4:7 ESV

Beloved, let us love one another, for love is from God, and whoever loves has been born of God and knows God.

Rainbow Reflection:
Go Out Into the World Today
and Say "Hello"

Drew will strike up a conversation with almost everyone he meets. Without any reservation, he often waves awkwardly and loudly says "Hello."

Most everyone smiles in response, and they start a conversation that generally adds joy to their day.

SCRIPTURE SUPPORT: 2 TIMOTHY 1:7 ESV

For God gave us a spirit not of fear but of power and love and self-control.

Rainbow Reflection:
Find Your Passion

When Drew was ten years old, I was struggling. I recognized that time to "catch up" to his peers was slipping away. His classmates were no longer learning to read, but rather reading to learn. They were exploring chapter books and subject matter that was well beyond Drew's level.

My dear friend Julie knew I was struggling and gave me her appointment for a healing massage. I was delighted and looked forward to the rest and relaxation that I was sure this would provide.

When I got to the appointment, the therapist addressed me as Julie. I explained to her that I was not Julie, that my name was Kathy and that my friend had generously given me her appointment for the massage.

The therapist welcomed me and went on to explain that her massage sessions include spiritual energy and healing touch. She shared that she had previously been a nun but had a calling to healing touch therapy. She continued to describe the session when she stopped mid-sentence and asked, "I'm sorry but I have to ask; do you have a child with special needs?"

I was so confused, as I had not told her anything about my family and she was not the least bit familiar with me, as she was expecting my friend Julie for the appointment.

I replied, "Why do you ask?"

She went on to say, "As I sit here talking with you, I am overcome with an image of a young man who was in a plane crash and suffered severe head injuries, but he was not ready to go. He felt he had more to do on earth and I get the sense that this is your son."

I was speechless and overwhelmed about what I was hearing.

I told her about Drew and his diagnosis of cognition delay. While I thought her vision was spectacular, I went on about my life as normal until after a trip to Hawaii forced me to revisit the discussion.

In Hawaii we stayed at a resort that had a children's movie theater and they planned to show the documentary *Drew Gets It*, which is a twenty-minute documentary film about Drew's message of love.

We were honored and excited to show the film and it was a great night.

Upon returning home, I was going through our photos and could not believe my eyes. The image below is of Drew and me before going into the theater. Drew's head is significantly affected and mimics the injuries that the therapist had described.

To this day I am not sure what all this means, but I do know that Drew is on a mission and is passionate and intentional about sharing his message of love.

SCRIPTURE SUPPORT: 1 CORINTHIANS 13:13

So now faith, hope, and love abide, these three; but the greatest of these is love.

Rainbow Reflection:
Have Faith in Everlasting Life

Lynn was a friend of mine and a student teacher who happened to tutor Drew in the second grade. He loved Ms. Lynn and responded to her beautifully. After a particularly tough conference with Drew's primary teacher regarding Drew's "deficits," I walked to my car deflated and discouraged as I fought back tears.

Lynn had recognized I left the conference upset and raced to follow me out to the parking lot.

I felt a tap on my shoulder and turned around. "Kathy, I'm so sorry how that difficult news about Drew's development was delivered. But I want you to know that if either of my girls came home with Andrew as a suitor, I would consider myself so lucky that they had selected such a loving and wonderful young man. Please never forget that he has boundless and special gifts."

She hugged me, and her encouraging words have carried me through many difficult moments in his life.

Fast forward five years and Drew and I are in the car running errands when my phone rings. A friend says she has difficult news and I should pull over. I hear the dread in her voice. She whispers through tears that our good friend and Andrew's tutor, Lynn, suddenly and unexpectedly died in her sleep.

I put my head down on my steering wheel and sob.

Drew is worried and asks, "What is the matter?"

How do I tell him that his beloved teacher is gone? How do I explain the death of such a vibrant young woman? I look at him through tears and begin to explain, "Drew, I am so sorry to tell you and I'm not exactly sure how to tell you, but Ms. Lynn has died."

Drew looks down, closes his eyes and is silent. After less than a minute, he looks at me with such assured confidence.

"It is okay, Mommy. She is happy; she is with Jesus."

From that moment on, Drew has remembered Lynn with fond and loving memories and a certainty that she is just fine.

SCRIPTURE SUPPORT: JOHN 3:16 ESV

For God so loved the world, that he gave his only Son, that whoever believes in him should not perish but have eternal life.

Rainbow Reflection:
Feel Support in the Spiritual

Although Drew's tutor, Ms. Lynn, has passed, she continues to show Drew support. On the day that we wrapped our home with his rainbows, a knock at the front door opened to my friend Nicole. She was holding a beautiful bouquet of rainbow balloons that she felt compelled to bring for this important day.

Nicole was a close friend to Ms. Lynn and said, "These balloons are a gift from Lynn, who is smiling down from heaven because she is so proud of Drew."

The balloons were a focal point of the day, and we knew that Lynn was lovingly with the boy she had so patiently tutored.

SCRIPTURE SUPPORT: LUKE 4:10 ESV

For it is written, "He will command his angels concerning you, to guard you."

Rainbow Reflection: Be Yourself

Drew's friend John has Williams syndrome. He is very open about his diagnosis and is confident and comfortable in his skin.

John went to Purcell Marion High School in Cincinnati, Ohio. This is a coed private Catholic school and the school's mascot is the Cavalier. Each year one senior is awarded the "Cavalier Award." This award honors a senior who has exemplifies high morals, dedication, and generosity among other desirable characteristics.

As a freshman, John would look in awe at the plaques displayed of past recipients of the Cavalier Award. At lunch he commented to his friends, "Do you guys see those plaques on the wall? I just hope to make a small difference in the school." John had no idea he was speaking something into prophecy.

John worked hard and did his best at Purcell Marion. He did everything with a positive attitude, determination, and was always available to help another. He kept his goal set on making a small difference in the school.

Senior awards night arrived, and John was called up to the podium. He was in disbelief when he was awarded the Cavalier Award.

"I couldn't believe my ears and it felt like I won a Grammy or a WWE award! I'd always daydreamed about seeing my name on one of those plaques, but I never really thought it would happen. I guess I just kept on being me, which was enough!"

John was the first individual with exceptionalities to win the award and made history for the special education program.

SCRIPTURE SUPPORT: ROMANS 12:2

Do not be conformed to this world, but be transformed by the renewal of your mind, that by testing you may discern what is the will of God, what is good and acceptable and perfect.

Rainbow Reflection:
Be Hopeful

Drew is forever an optimist and a diehard fan of the Cincinnati Bengals and the Cincinnati Reds. Even when the Bengals are having a dismal season, he never loses hope and bravely declares, "Today's the day, Mommy; the Bengals are going to bring home a win!"

SCRIPTURE SUPPORT: ROMANS 12:12

Rejoice in hope, be patient in tribulation, be constant in prayer.

Rainbow Reflection:
Stay Close to God

Drew has a friendship with God. He often talks about God as if he is physically present.

"I miss Jesus; how many days until church?"

SCRIPTURE SUPPORT: ROMANS 8:28

And we know that for those who love God all things work together for good, for those who are called according to his purpose.

Rainbow Reflection:
Be Mindful of Labels

You have probably noticed the word "exceptionalities" used throughout this book. That is an intentional shift from the word "disabilities," which is the commonly used word to describe people with exceptionalities.

The prefix "dis" means apart, away, a negative or reversing force. Furthermore, the informal verb meaning of "dis" means to disrespect or to talk negatively.

None of these associations remotely describe this community. In fact, words such as insightful, fun, loving, and positive are more accurate descriptors.

This community is exceptional.

The reference to "individuals with exceptionalities" describes this community more accurately and what they contribute to make the world a better place.

SCRIPTURE SUPPORT: ISAIAH 41:10 ESV

Fear not, for I am with you; be not dismayed, for I am your God; I will strengthen you, I will help you, I will uphold you with my righteous right hand.

Rainbow Reflection: Invite Interaction, as You May Never Know the Lasting Impact

In September of 2017, the short documentary *Drew Gets It* was invited to be in the Niagara International Film Festival.

Our family attended the film festival and stayed at a lovely hotel near the falls. A short walk, and you could begin to hear the spectacular waterfalls which generally includes a rainbow due to the interaction of the water and light.

At the hotel, Drew made friends with Kofi, one of the hotel employees in reception. Each morning during our short stay, he and Drew would spend a few minutes chatting.

I realized they enjoyed talking, but what I didn't realize was the impact of that interaction. Upon checking out, Kofi told us that he was a poet and was inspired to write a poem for Drew.

YOU'RE SPECIAL

Drew's – Bow
It was all void until
I saw in your eyes, eight colors:
Love, Joy, Peace,
Endurance, Kindness, Goodness, Faithfulness, and Drew.
Filled with living water
Inhaling, exhaling hope,
To quench the thirst of a thirsty world
When you wrapped your
Kaleidoscopic arms around me
Assuring me, I can cope, I found me
In the refuge of God's own presence.
I wish I could say I met an angel,
Celestial and glorious
But what I saw in your eyes
Supersedes an angel
A halo of countless rainbows
Crowning your head.
Dedicated to Drew
Written by Kofi Dedenyo

SCRIPTURE SUPPORT: PSALM 103:20-21 ESV

Bless the LORD, O you his angels, you mighty ones who do his word, obeying the voice of his word! Bless the LORD, all his hosts, his ministers, who do his will!

Rainbow Reflection:
Be Cheerful

One frustrating afternoon, Drew simply says, "Cheer up; it will all work out, because God says so." He is always so trusting and full of love.

SCRIPTURE SUPPORT: PROVERBS 4:23 ESV

Keep your heart with all vigilance, for from it flow the springs of life.

Rainbow Reflection:
Love All God's Creatures

Drew has a sixth sense about animals. On road trips, he spots animals quickly when I never see them, and he has a passion for the Cincinnati Zoo. His collection of animal toy figurines is up to 150 and growing.

"I love animals because I can touch them and that makes me feel like I can experience a connection."

SCRIPTURE SUPPORT: GENESIS 1:24 ESV

And God said, "Let the earth bring forth living creatures according to their kinds—livestock and creeping things and beasts of the earth according to their kinds." And it was so.

Rainbow Reflection:
Ask Forgiveness

Drew may be cognitively delayed, but he rarely forgets his manners. In the instances when it is needed, he never forgets to say, "I'm sorry, Mommy."

SCRIPTURE SUPPORT: EPHESIANS 4:32 ESV

Be kind to one another, tenderhearted, forgiving one another,
as God in Christ forgave you.

Rainbow Reflection: Believe in Yourself

Nothing stops Elaina. If she wants to accomplish something; she gets it done! "Even though I'm a little person, I feel like if I put my mind to it, I can do anything."

SCRIPTURE SUPPORT: JOB 42:2 ESV

"I know that you can do all things, and that no purpose of yours can be thwarted."

Rainbow Reflection:
Let It Be

By the time Drew was five, a comprehensive team of "experts" determined he was cognitively delayed and the outcome for his development would be greatly limited. This news was so difficult to hear, and denial was my immediate response.

The day after hearing the news, I went to a spiritual retreat. Part of the agenda included the opportunity to go to confession. I decided to go and elected to confess face to face with the priest.

I had barely sat down when the priest asked, "What is weighing heavy on your heart?"

I responded, "Nothing, Father, I am here to confess."

He repeated, "What is weighing heavy on your heart?"

It was as if he could see the burden I was trying so earnestly to cover up and once again but through building tears and a shaky voice, I responded, "Nothing, Father, I am here to confess."

The kind priest said, "I get the sense that you need to talk more than you need to confess."

I could not believe how he saw into my heart. I put my face in my hands and just cried without talking for several minutes. I finally collected myself and managed to tell him the harsh news and dismal predictions that had been made about my sweet little five-year-old son. I told him I was sad, angry, and frustrated that "experts" could put such limitations on a child only five years out of the womb!

He looked at me with such sensitivity and assurance. "You were meant to see me today. I am from a large family and the gem and shining star of the family is our dear sister who has Down syndrome." He went on, "You have been given a wonderful gift, and your son will be a joy to you and to many others."

He encouraged me to find inspiration from Mary, another mother who was told difficult news that was hard to hear. He retold the story about the angels who announced to Mary she was with child, yet she had never been with a man nor was even married.

He said, "She too was probably in denial, confused, and scared--but quickly responded to her calling with a resounding Yes!" The priest gave me a hug and said, "Let it be."

It took me awhile to accept, as I was determined to "fix" everything. How much easier and smoother life would have been if I had simply trusted in our Lord.

SCRIPTURE SUPPORT: LUKE 1:38 ESV

And Mary said, "Behold, I am the servant of the Lord; let it be to me according to your word," and the angel departed from her.

Rainbow Reflection: Even When the World Feels Dark, Know That You Are Loved

On a particularly tough day, Drew walked into my office and found me sad. I hadn't heard him walk in but what I did hear was what he whispered in my ear: "It is okay, Mommy. God loves you."

SCRIPTURE SUPPORT: 1 JOHN 4:8

Anyone who does not love does not know God, because God is love.

JANUARY 22

Rainbow Reflection: Do Something Thoughtful and Unexpected

Drew loves nothing more than to pass out his "You're Special" rainbow cards. When he gives one to a stranger, I usually feel compelled to provide some context, but some days I don't have the energy.

On one of those days, Drew reminded me of the importance of his small acts of kindness.

"I love to surprise people because it makes them smile and makes them feel happy."

SCRIPTURE SUPPORT: PSALMS 90:14 ESV

Satisfy us in the morning with your steadfast love,
that we may rejoice and be glad all our days.

Rainbow Reflection: Take Comfort in Salvation and Eternal Light

On a family road trip to the beach, we break up the trip with a hotel stay. The hotel property includes a breakfast bar and Drew is wide awake at 7:00 a.m. and ready to be "Mr. Social." He smiles and waves to everyone, Forrest Gump style, whether they are ready to interact or not so early in the morning.

I am quietly making his plate when he spots one woman who is wearing an Alabama Roll Tide t-shirt and because Drew LOVES sports, the Alabama t-shirt is all the encouragement he needs to strike up a conversation.

He lights up and says, "Is that your favorite team? Do you think they are going to win?" They chit chat for a while and Drew says, "We are going on vacation to meet all of our cousins at the beach and to have so much fun. Why are you at the hotel?"

The woman gets quiet, looks down and then looks back up with tears in her eyes and says, "Actually, I am here for my mamma's funeral."

Drew gets very quiet and seems to reflect. In a few seconds, he says with confidence and clarity, *"It's alright. You don't need to be sad; your mamma is in heaven."*

The woman has a look of relief and disbelief come over her face and she quietly whispers, "Thank you."

A bit later she seeks me out to say, "I want you to know I believe what your son told me, and those words of encouragement will get me through this very difficult day. It meant so much just when I needed it most; he is very special."

SCRIPTURE SUPPORT: LUKE 23:43 ESV

And he said to him, "Truly, I say to you, today you will be with me in Paradise."

Rainbow Reflection: Take the Time to See the Beauty in Something Today

Several times a week Drew excitedly calls me into the living room that faces west, to say, "Look at that sunset!" Usually it is **not** that spectacular, with only faint hues of pink and orange remaining. Yet, Drew just stares in wonderment at the beauty before his eyes. Only then, and through his eyes, do I see it too.

SCRIPTURE SUPPORT: ECCLESIASTES 3:11 ESV

He has made everything beautiful in its time.
Also, he has put eternity into man's heart,
yet so that he cannot find out what God has done
form the beginning to the end.

Rainbow Reflection: Share Kind Words With One Another

Often children with exceptionalities are very wise in different ways. Drew inherently knows to say kind words and to say them often.

"You make good food."

"I love you, Sissy."

"Grandma, thank you for playing with me."

"Daddy, you are so nice to take me for donuts."

"You look so pretty in your dress!"

"Mommy, you are my angel."

SCRIPTURE SUPPORT: COLOSSIANS 3:8 ESV

But now you must put them all away, anger, wrath, malice,
slander, and obscene talk from your mouth.

Rainbow Reflection:
Choose to Be Happy

It is amazing how often individuals with exceptionalities have the best outlook. Drew's dear friend Maria offers great perspective.

"When you are grumpy, maybe you should look inside. Be more positive and things might begin to go the way you want them to go."

SCRIPTURE SUPPORT: 1 THESSALONIANS 5:16-18 ESV

Rejoice always, pray without ceasing, give thanks in all circumstances; for this is the will of God in Christ Jesus for you.

Rainbow Reflection:
Encourage One Another

In NYC at Grand Central Station, Drew hands a stranger his rainbow card that says "You're Special." She asks, "Why did you give that to me?"

Drew replies, "I don't know, I guess I just wanted to remind you that you are special."

With tears in her eyes, she shares that lately she has been at a "breaking point" and this small encouragement from a stranger was just what she needed to feel loved. They hug and then go their separate ways.

SCRIPTURE SUPPORT: 1 THESSALONIANS 5:11 ESV

Therefore encourage one another and build one another up, just as you are doing.

JANUARY 28

Rainbow Reflection:
Have Faith and Trust

The day we wrapped the house with Drew's rainbows was a glorious day! People came from several states away. Neighbors, family, friends, and strangers filled our block to witness the rainbow-covered house. The news even came to cover the story.

As we completed the front of the house and it was covered in rainbows, we took a family photo, and just after the picture was captured, Drew sprinted with intention to the side of our home. He stopped and was looking up into our tree.

I was unsure why Drew would run away from the crowd and the excitement to look up at the tree. However, I was awestruck. Drew looked so peaceful and engaged, so much so that I pulled out my phone to snap a picture. A few moments later, his godfather approached Drew and they had a conversation and an embrace.

The day got busy and I did not think much more about this event until the next evening. As I tucked Drew in, I shared the picture I had captured and asked him why he had run over to the side of the house. He replied, "God called my name, so I ran over." He went on, "When I looked up, I saw Jesus who said, I like your rainbows and I am happy that you put them on your house for all to see." Drew continued, "Then Jesus came down and sat by me on the railing."

I was in disbelief and asked Drew what Jesus looked like. "Jesus was wearing a slash."

I was sure Drew was confused and meant sash. "I think you mean a sash, like the priests wear at church."

"No, Mommy, a slash," continued Drew.

I agreed to disagree and told him to have sweet dreams. After tucking Drew in, I called his godfather to ask what he remembered about the conversation. His godfather reiterated Drew's story and explained that Drew had told him he was talking to Jesus.

His godfather did not interpret this as literal and commented to Drew that he can always talk to Jesus because Jesus is in his heart.

Weeks later I was driving and thinking about the conversation with Drew when I gasped out loud. What if Drew did mean slash, referring to the wound inflicted by the Roman soldiers as Jesus was hanging on the cross? I begin to question myself. After all, Drew was the one who had the experience. Shame on me to doubt his explanation and to have such weak faith.

That evening I asked Drew about it again and asked if he meant "slash" like a cut in the skin. Drew went about playing and simply said, "Yes, Mommy, that is what I told you."

Interestingly, my maiden name is Thomas. Just like the Apostle Thomas doubted, I too doubted what my son was telling me.

SCRIPTURE SUPPORT: JOHN 20:29 ESV

Jesus said to him, "Have you believed because you have seen me? Blessed are those who have not seen and yet have believed."

Rainbow Reflection:
Encourage Someone Today

"**M**ommy, you are my angel from heaven."

"Drew, you have it all wrong; you are the angel."

"No, Mommy, you are the angel."

"No, Drew, you are the angel."

I am far from his ideal of me, but with his sweet words, I am encouraged, and I want to do better.

SCRIPTURE SUPPORT: PSALMS 28:7 ESV

The Lord is my strength and my shield in him my heart trusts, and I am helped; my heart exults, and with my song I give thanks to him.

JANUARY 30

Rainbow Reflection:
See Your Dreams Coming True

Dakota is quiet but speaks loudly through her artwork. She is a talented artist and communicates feelings and emotions with the characters and personas she creates from her imagination. The year her father unexpectedly died; she utilized her talent to work through her sorrow.

"I see my imagination in pictures and believe it can become my art."

SCRIPTURE SUPPORT: HEBREWS 11:1-3 ESV

Now faith is the assurance of things hoped for, the conviction of things not seen. For by it the people of old received their commendation. By faith we understand that the universe was created by the word of God, so that what is seen was not made out of things that are visible.

Rainbow Reflection: Push Your Comfort Level to "Step Out of Your Boat"

While on a family getaway to Chicago, we loaded onto an elevator on the 28th floor heading for the lobby, plenty of time for Drew to work his magic.

Elevators in general are a curious study in social behavior. Most people don't make eye contact and avoid talking or touching as they pull tighter into themselves. Attention is generally glued to the numbers above as the elevator descends floors: 28, 27, 26, 25.

That is, unless you are Drew.

Drew had his eye on the prize. He had already scanned the elevator smiling and waving to everyone and managed to pick the most foreboding individual on the elevator to chat with. I held my breath, thinking, *Oh Drew, not him—anyone else on the elevator but him.*

This man was handsome, tall, finely dressed, but completely unapproachable. He wore a serious if not gruff expression, and one could tell he was a man of importance, a man on a mission and a man not to be bothered.

Drew stared up at the businessman, who was doing his best to ignore Drew; however, with a confident and much too loud voice for the crammed elevator, Drew asked, "Do you like hot dogs?"

Hushed laughter broke out in the crowded elevator, immediately easing the tension.

A bit annoyed, the businessman responded, "Uh, yeah, I guess."

Well, that was just the encouragement Drew needed, and his non-stop chatter began. "I like hot dogs, I like Chicago pizza, do you like pizza, I like the Cubs, we are staying in Chicago, do you like Chicago, I like Chicago."

The serious businessman couldn't help himself; he drank the Drew Kool-Aid. A small smile spread across his face and his stiff shoulders dropped as he succumbed to Drew's persistent charm.

By the time we made it down 27 floors, the entire mood of the elevator had shifted from uncomfortable silence to camaraderie.

The staunch and unapproachable businessman got off the elevator with a skip in his step. A reset button had been pushed and his day was better off for having spent time with Drew.

While walking away he called, "Hey buddy, have fun today in Chicago, and it was so nice to meet you."

Drew had worked his magic.

SCRIPTURE SUPPORT: MATTHEW 14:28-30 ESV

And Peter answered him, "Lord, if it is you, command me to come to you on the water." He said, "Come." So, Peter got out of the boat and walked on the water and came to Jesus.

Rainbow Reflection:
Affirm What You Want to Happen Today

"Today is going to be a great day!" Andrew shouts as he saunters into the kitchen upon waking up.

SCRIPTURE SUPPORT: JOHN 17:17 ESV

Sanctify them in the truth; your word is truth.

Rainbow Reflection:
Go For It!

I sit in awe of Drew's passion to achieve, "Ba Bam! Look at that! I got it done; I did it!"

SCRIPTURE SUPPORT: COLOSSIANS 3:23 ESV

Whatever you do, work heartily, as for the Lord and not for men.

Rainbow Reflection:
Listen and Hear

Some days it can feel like a "new day, same Drew." Change and progress come very slowly, and most days include the same conversations about sports, timelines, and routines. I know that at times, I am guilty of half listening.

Drew recognizes and asks, "Do you hear me, Mommy?"

I feel guilty and reflect that I owe him the same attention as I would others despite the monotony of the topic, because he deserves my full attention.

SCRIPTURE SUPPORT: PROVERBS 18:13

If one gives an answer before he hears, it is his folly and shame.

FEBRUARY 4

Rainbow Reflection: Elevate One Another

I have witnessed that children with exceptionalities are never short on compliments, such as: "Grandma, I don't see any wings on your back, but you are my angel."

SCRIPTURE SUPPORT: 1 CORINTHIANS 2:9

But, as it is written, "What no eye has seen, nor ear heard, nor the heart of man imagined, what God has prepared for those who love him."

Rainbow Reflection:
Give 100%

So often many of us feel like we are never enough, but Drew demonstrates perseverance and a sense of accomplishment at even the smallest achievements. "You should go out and try your hardest and never give up. I didn't think I'd ever learn to tie my shoes and then just like that, one day, I did it!"

SCRIPTURE SUPPORT: 2 TIMOTHY 2:15

Do your best to present yourself to God as one approved, a worker who has no need to be ashamed, rightly handling the word of truth.

Rainbow Reflection:
Protect What You Love

Drew often believes he has the superpowers of his movie heroes. He believes that the light sabers in Star Wars are real and that he can spin a web like Spider Man.

"Mommy, if someone tried to hurt our family, I would fight them with my light saber."

SCRIPTURE SUPPORT: PSALMS 138:7 ESV

"Though I walk in the midst of trouble, you preserve my life, you stretch out your hand against the wrath of my enemies, and your right hand delivers me."

Rainbow Reflection: Ask Someone to Play

A dear cousin with dwarfism reminds us of the importance of inclusion for everyone. "I have been lonely before and then a friend asked me to play; you show friendship by asking someone to play."

How insightful and valuable to remember that at all ages and stages we need to invite others to "play."

SCRIPTURE SUPPORT: COLOSSIANS 2:2 ESV

That their hearts may be encouraged, being knit together in love, to reach all the riches of full assurance of understanding and the knowledge of God's mystery, which is Christ.

Rainbow Reflection:
See People

Drew's friend John, who has Williams syndrome, adheres to a personal mantra that a disability should not define you. He says "disability" is just a word and believes that others are often insecure around people with disabilities.

"When people are open to people with disabilities, they are more open to seeing us. Before they know it, they don't even see our disabilities. They become more understanding."

"As others spend time with me and get to know me, they don't even see my disability; they just see John."

SCRIPTURE SUPPORT: HEBREWS 13:2 ESV

Do not neglect to show hospitality to strangers, for thereby some have entertained angels unawares.

Rainbow Reflection: Compliment One Another

To be acknowledged, recognized, or thanked are simple ways to let another know how they are appreciated, and so often I've noticed that individuals with exceptionalities excel in this skill. One of my favorite daily rainbows was one that said, "I like your food." Drew loves to eat and is always so appreciative of meals. His simple phrase is just the encouragement needed to make cooking daily dinners worthwhile.

SCRIPTURE SUPPORT: 1 THESSALONIANS 5:18 ESV

Give thanks in all circumstances; for this is the will of God in Christ Jesus for you.

Rainbow Reflection:
Dream for Yourself

From a little boy to current day, Drew dreams big! At twenty-three, he still declares, "When I grow up, I think I will probably be a quarterback for the Cincinnati Bengals."

SCRIPTURE SUPPORT: PROVERBS 16:3 ESV

Commit your work to the Lord, and your plans will be established.

Rainbow Reflection:
Find What Works for You to Decompress

Many individuals with exceptionalities seem to know how to self soothe and calm themselves. I've seen children flap their hands, hop up and down and even rock themselves. One of Drew's friends created her own little world with music and movement.

"Whenever I feel scared or upset, I twirl a lot and I call it dream twirling."

SCRIPTURE SUPPORT: PHILIPPIANS 4:6 ESV

Do not be anxious about anything, but in everything by prayer and supplication with thanksgiving let your request be made know to God.

FEBRUARY 12

Rainbow Reflection: Care for Others in Words and Actions

From a very early age and to this day, Drew has always wanted to protect and care for others. In fact, whenever we are in a group, it is Drew who ensures that the slowest one among us is never far behind. I often overhear him telling his sisters, grandmother, and even his pet dog Maggie, "Don't worry, I'll take care of you."

SCRIPTURE SUPPORT: PHILIPPIANS 2:4 ESV

Let each of you look not only to his own interests,
but also to the interests of others.

Rainbow Reflection:
Know Yourself

It makes Drew uncomfortable for things to be out of order. In fact, I am confident that he has a mental scan of his room. He cannot rest or relax if things are out of place.

One night after tucking him in, I bumped a toy shark as I was leaving his room. He abruptly sat up and asked, "Mommy, did you bump my shark?"

I replied, "I did, Drew, but I fixed it."

I walked out of his room but quietly stood around the corner predicting what would happen next. Once Drew thought I had gone, I heard him scrambling out of bed toward the shark to make sure it was exactly back as it had been before. Once he was reassured that things were "exactly" as they should be, Drew was able to relax to sleep.

SCRIPTURE SUPPORT: 1 THESSALONIANS 5:19

Do not quench the Spirit.

Rainbow Reflection:
Remember That Love Is the Answer

Drew is perplexed and upset when he hears of fighting or violence. He often questions the behavior and says, "I don't know why it is so hard for people to get along. God just wants us to love one another."

SCRIPTURE SUPPORT: 1 JOHN 4:11 ESV

Beloved, if God so loved us, we also ought to love one another.

FEBRUARY 15

Rainbow Reflection: Be There for Others

Pets are known to be man's best friend, and that has certainly held true for Drew. Our Goldendoodle, Maggie, has been his companion and best buddy for fifteen years. As she was aging, she greatly slowed down and struggled to get up. I would often find Drew holding her as he rubbed her head and whispered, "It's okay, old girl. I got you; I'm here for you."

SCRIPTURE SUPPORT: 2 TIMOTHY 2:3 ESV

Share in suffering as a good soldier of Christ Jesus.

Rainbow Reflection:
Remember That by Helping Others,
We Also Help Ourselves

When volunteering in Dayton to help those affected by a tornado, Drew commented, "I wanted to cheer people up, but they cheered me up too." He reminded me that volunteering is good for the soul and as powerful for the volunteer as it is for the cause.

SCRIPTURE SUPPORT: ACTS 20:35 ESV

In all things I have shown you that by working hard in this way we must help the weak and remember the words of the Lord Jesus, how he himself said, "It is more blessed to give than to receive."

Rainbow Reflection: Look Close and See the Beauty in Everyone

Drew leaves a gathering of friends and upon getting into the car he states, "Sarah is so pretty; isn't she, Mom?" Interestingly, Sarah has many complications that have drastically affected her physical appearance. Most would not look at her and remark about her physical beauty.

Drew, however, is smiling ear to ear thinking about their friendship and the fun they share. He sees her, the inner beauty and the warm smile that is ever-present on her face. He sees his friend.

SCRIPTURE SUPPORT: 1 PETER 3:3-4 ESV

Do not let your adoring be external - the braiding of hair and putting on of gold jewelry, or the clothing you wear - but let your adorning be the hidden person of the heart with the imperishable beauty of a gentle and quiet spirit, which in God's sight is very precious.

Rainbow Reflection:
Reach Out a Hand

A volunteer at an event recognized she was experiencing the signs of a panic attack. Her heart was pounding, and her palms were sweaty. Disappointed, she prepared to leave.

As she stood up, she was met with a genuine smile and a rainbow drawing. Drew had noticed and handed her one of his "You're Special" cards.

Once he handed her the rainbow, she thought to herself, *I can do this!*

She reflected that this was the encouragement she needed to get through the moment.

Drew's simple gesture and support was just what she needed, and today they are friends.

SCRIPTURE SUPPORT: 1 JOHN 4:11 ESV

Beloved, if God so loved us, we also ought to love one another.

Rainbow Reflection:
Choose Peace Today

Sometimes individuals with exceptionalities say so much by saying so little. "In London, I made a new friend by giving him a rainbow; it is so easy to make friends."

SCRIPTURE SUPPORT: ROMANS 12:17 ESV

Repay no one evil for evil but give thought to do
what is honorable in the sight of all.

Rainbow Reflection: Marvel in God's Works

Drew and his friends notice everything. Small everyday occasions stir up excitement and wonder. "Hurry up and just look at all of the stars; they are so pretty!"

They remind us to slow down to take in the beauty of everyday life.

SCRIPTURE SUPPORT: PSALMS 8 3-4 ESV

When I look at your heavens, the work of your fingers, the moon and the stars, which you have set in place, what is man that you are mindful of him, and the son of many that you care for him.

Rainbow Reflection:
Greet Someone Joyfully Today

Coming home from a long trip, I was so excited to see my family. As I approached the baggage claim, I wondered if they would be with my father-in-law, who was to pick me up at the airport. As soon as the thought entered my mind, I noticed a six-foot male jumping up and down and realized it was Drew. He was waving his hands screaming, "Mommy, Mommy!" with no inhibitions or regard for who saw him, how he sounded or how he looked. His physical size and appearance are a disconnect to his seven-year-old cognition, but his sheer joy brought smiles to strangers. His innocent exuberance was contagious.

SCRIPTURE SUPPORT: PROVERBS 17:22 ESV

A joyful heart is good medicine, but a crushed spirit dries up the bones.

Rainbow Reflection: Allow Yourself Time to Be Sad and Then Move Forward

A good friend of Drew's, with a similar exceptionality, recently lost a parent and was deep in grief. However, after a short time, she was doing much better. When asked how she was managing, she said, "I got all the tears out and then I felt better." She went on to say, "You don't have to hold in your tears; it is okay to cry." She added, "I just listen to my heart and my body and then I feel better. I still get sad sometimes, but I take time to cry or feel sad and afterwards I feel lighter."

Once again it hit me how simple yet powerful her advice was to me. I thought how often I am so busy trying to "solve" that I make too much noise to even hear my own mind and heart.

SCRIPTURE SUPPORT:

The Lord is near to the brokenhearted and saves the crushed in spirit.

Rainbow Reflection: Have Faith

Drew is so relaxed and trusting in his faith. "When I am scared, I say, God and Saint Michael, please watch over me and then I don't worry anymore."

SCRIPTURE SUPPORT: PSALMS 4:8 ESV

In peace I will both lie down and sleep; for you alone,
O Lord, make me dwell in safety.

Rainbow Reflection:
Be Creative and Do Not Be Inhibited

So often we are held back by fear. We doubt and question which can lead to shutting down or giving up. I am inspired how often individuals with exceptionalities just go for it and often have such confidence when trying new things. Dakota, a friend with exceptionalities, confidently exclaims, "I just decided to be an artist because it is interesting to put your imagination into drawings."

SCRIPTURE SUPPORT: EXODUS 35:31 ESV

And he has filled him with the Spirit of God, with skill, with intelligence, with knowledge, and with all craftsmanship, to devise artistic designs, to work in gold and silver and bronze.

Rainbow Reflection: Trust in Faith

Individuals with exceptionalities seem to have a knack for simplifying such complex topics. Our cousin, Doug, with exceptionalities comments, "If I could talk to God, I'd ask him if I could live a long and happy life and then go to heaven."

SCRIPTURE SUPPORT: LUKE 12:32 ESV

"Fear not, little flock, for it is your Father's good pleasure to give you the kingdom."

FEBRUARY 26

Rainbow Reflection: Get to Know People

People are generally open to meeting and interacting with people who are different. In fact, it is often considered exciting to get to know individuals with unique backgrounds and to learn about new cultures. However, some individuals with exceptionalities feel that others are intimidated or afraid to approach them, yet they yearn to be included and understood. A friend with Williams syndrome shares, "When people talk to me, I think it opens their minds. They understand that people with exceptionalities have a lot to offer when they get to know us."

SCRIPTURE SUPPORT: PSALMS 145:9 ESV

The Lord is good to all, and his mercy is over all that he has made.

Rainbow Reflection:
Set Goals

While the voice in my head often sees barriers, challenges, or obstacles, Drew almost always sees possibilities.

"I need to learn more about animals, because the Cincinnati zoo might need me to be a zookeeper."

SCRIPTURE SUPPORT: PROVERBS 16:9 ESV

The heart of man plans his way, but the Lord establishes his steps.

Rainbow Reflection:
Be of Service to Someone Today

"**D**addy is so nice to me and helps me shave and look handsome so I like to help him. I like to ask him, "How can I help you, Daddy?"

SCRIPTURE SUPPORT: ACTS 20:35 ESV

In all things I have shown you that by working hard in this way we must help the weak and remember the words of the Lord Jesus, how he himself said, "It is more blessed to give than to receive."

Rainbow Reflection: Believe in Yourself

Drew believes in people and generally rejects self-doubt or negative thoughts.

It's 6:00 a.m. in our kitchen, and I'm waking up slowly. Drew bounds down the steps and I'm not quite ready for all of his energy.

"Good morning, Mommy, how is my mommy?"

"To be honest, Drew, today I'm kind of tired."

Drew puts his hands on my shoulders, looks me in the eye and with such confidence says, "No, Mommy, you can go out and be pretty all day long."

With his solid belief in me, he convinces me to do just that!

SCRIPTURE SUPPORT: 1 CORINTHIANS 9:23 ESV

Do you not know that in a race all the runners run, but only one receives the prize? So, run that you may obtain it.

Rainbow Reflection:
Take Quiet Time for Yourself

The awareness and introspective nature of some individuals with exceptionalities is astounding. A classmate with Down syndrome comments, "When I feel nervous or scared, I need to take time to myself. Sometimes it is good to be alone."

SCRIPTURE SUPPORT: MATTHEW 6:6

But when you pray, go into your room and shut the door and pray to your Father who is in secret. And your Father who sees in secret will reward you.

MARCH 2

Rainbow Reflection: Think Positive Thoughts

Instead of complicating life, keep it simple and take the advice of Maria, an exceptional individual and one of Drew's best friends. "When I feel sad, I think about something that makes me happy and then I feel better."

SCRIPTURE SUPPORT: PHILIPPIANS 4:8

Finally, brothers, whatever is true, whatever is honorable, whatever is just, whatever is pure, whatever is lovely, whatever is commendable, if there is any excellence, if there is anything worthy of praise, think about these things.

MARCH 3

Rainbow Reflection: Shelter with Love

Like most people, individuals with exceptionalities appreciate a safe haven and like to be a safe haven for one another. A friend with Asperger syndrome shares, "I feel safe at Grandma and Grandpa's house."

SCRIPTURE SUPPORT: PSALMS 27:1 ESV

The Lord is my light and my salvation; whom shall I fear? The Lord is the stronghold of my life; of whom shall I be afraid?

Rainbow Reflection: Lift Others Up

Drew was so fortunate to make a great group of friends through the Cougar Football program during elementary school. Years later and as young adults, these young men still call, visit, and elevate Drew whenever they see him.

Enthusiastically, Drew exclaims, "When I see my old Cougar football buddies, I feel so excited. Friends are a good thing to have."

Recently I reached out to thank Evan, who is now a college graduate and still regularly calls Drew and takes him on outings. During the call Evan was quick to tell me that he gets more out of the visits than Drew does. He said, "Drew lifts me up."

SCRIPTURE SUPPORT: PSALMS 30:11 ESV

You have turned for me my mourning into dancing,
you have loosed my sackcloth and clothed me with gladness

MARCH 5

Rainbow Reflection: Make Time for Loved Ones

Drew recognizes the gift of family and friends. Excitedly he says, "Today we are spending the day together. Family is my favorite and I love it when the whole family is together."

SCRIPTURE SUPPORT: MATTHEW 18:20

For where two or three are gathered in my name, there am I among them.

Rainbow Reflection:
Acknowledge Your Gifts and Talents

It seems more common to see our faults versus our gifts. Drew has taught me to recognize what one does well and to be grateful. He confidently and proudly declares, "I'm most proud of my rainbow drawings."

SCRIPTURE SUPPORT: JAMES 1:17 ESV

Every good gift and every perfect gift is from above, coming down from the Father of lights with whom there is no variation of shadow due to change.

Rainbow Reflection:
Treat Yourself

When it comes to treating oneself, Drew and his friends do it with no regret! Preparing for an ice cream eating contest, Drew comments, "When I think of eating ice cream, I feel pretty happy."

SCRIPTURE SUPPORT: PSALMS 37:4 ESV

Delight yourself in the Lord, and he will give you the desires of your heart.

Rainbow Reflection:
Be Someone's Cheerleader Today

From age six, Drew has been on swim team. It is a typical swim team, so he is up against tough competition, but year after year he goes for it and never gives up.

When the blow horn sounds, Drew is generally grinning ear to ear and waving as he is about to jump off the block. Due to his sensory integration, Drew will not put his face in the water, and he generally finishes last by 1-2 laps.

This is where the magic happens and his determination kicks in. At almost every swim meet, crowds gather at each end of the lane to encourage Drew and cheer him on to the finish. Often the entire natatorium is shouting, "Go Drew, go Drew!" People who've never met Drew and kids from other teams become his biggest fans.

Spectators are motivated by his will, drive, and sheer joy at being involved. Drew often says, "I saw the kids at the end of the swim lane cheering for me, so I kept going."

SCRIPTURE SUPPORT: PHILIPPIANS 3:14 ESV

I press on toward the goal for the price of the upward call of God in Christ Jesus.

Rainbow Reflection:
Pray for Others

Drew always remembers his prayers. "Mommy, I prayed to the angels and God to keep you safe when you are on the airplane."

SCRIPTURE SUPPORT: PSALMS 12:7 ESV

You, O Lord, will keep them; you will guard us from this generation forever.

MARCH 10

Rainbow Reflection: Follow Your Passion

Every human has a passion, and individuals with exceptionalities have taught me to go after my dreams with affirmation. One of Drew's friends explained that the passion in his heart is God speaking to him. So often I've overheard declarations:

"I want to become an artist."

"I want to win the Cavalier award."

"I want to be a cheerleader."

"I want to entertain like Elvis."

Drew recently whispered to me in church, "My biggest dream is to be a sportscaster on ESPN."

It occurred to me that so often we simply don't declare the dreams held closest to our hearts.

SCRIPTURE SUPPORT: PROVERBS 3:5-6 ESV

Trust in the Lord with all your heart, and do not lean on your own understanding.
In all your ways acknowledge him, and he will make straight your paths.

Rainbow Reflection: Never Underestimate the Impact of Saying "Thank You"

Drew went to a Cubs game and was invited to go onto the field. It was a great day, and he was so happy and thankful. Upon returning home, Drew decided to write a thank you note and included a rainbow card for the Cubs staff.

About a week later we got an email from the staff with images attached. They had written, "You're Special DrewsRainbows.org" and "Cubs sign Drew Leurck" on the Wrigley Field jumbotron! He was so excited but curious as to when he would need to show up for practice now that he was part of the team!

SCRIPTURE SUPPORT: PSALMS 105:1 ESV

Oh, give thanks to the Lord; call upon his name;
make known his deeds among the peoples!

Rainbow Reflection:
Address One Another With Endearment

At twenty-three, Drew still often says "Mommy and Daddy." At his age, I should probably encourage him to say "Mom and Dad," but what is the point? In those words, there is so much love.

SCRIPTURE SUPPORT: 1 CORINTHIANS 13:1-9 ESV

If I speak in the tongues of men and of angels, but have not love, I am a noisy gong or a clanging cymbal. And if I have prophetic powers, and understand all mysteries and all knowledge, and if I have all faith, so as to remove mountains, but have not love, I am nothing. If I give away all I have, and I deliver up my body to be burned, but have not love, I gain nothing.

Rainbow Reflection:
Keep the Conversation Going with God

Drew's relationship with God is so simple and matter of fact. "I'm going to bed now so I can talk to Jesus."

SCRIPTURE SUPPORT: PSALMS 17:6

I call upon you, for you will answer me, O God;
incline your ear to me; hear my words.

MARCH 14

Rainbow Reflection: Honor Elders

Drew makes friends easily, and one day after church he introduced me to Ms. Martha, whom he just met.

"This is Ms. Martha, and she is going to be ninety-one; can we make her a card?"

That week we did exactly that and when we delivered it to Ms. Martha, she smiled so big and said, "Drew, I am just so tickled that you remembered and took the time to make me a rainbow."

After further discussion with Ms. Martha, we learned that she is a retired special needs teacher. She shared that getting Drew's handmade card felt like a birthday wish from all the special students she had taught. God works in beautiful ways.

SCRIPTURE SUPPORT: 1 TIMOTHY 5:1 ESV

Do not rebuke an older man but encourage him as you would a father, younger men as brothers.

MARCH 15

Rainbow Reflection: Take Time Out for Your Hobbies and Passions

Drew is passionate about sports and has gratitude for the joy they provide. He says, "Sports is my thing; I like to watch all the sports because they make me happy. Thank you, Jesus, for sports!"

SCRIPTURE SUPPORT: 1 CORINTHIANS 10:31

So, whether you eat or drink, or whatever you do, do all to the glory of God

MARCH 16

Rainbow Reflection: Dream Big

Drew reminds me that at any age we have potential and should dream because we never stop growing and changing. At age twenty-three, Drew still dreams about when he grows up. "Maybe when I grow up, I'll be a horse jockey in the Kentucky Derby!"

SCRIPTURE SUPPORT: LUKE 1:37 ESV

For nothing will be impossible with God.

Rainbow Reflection:
Always Be a Kid at Heart

For Drew, the rhythm of life is often measured from event to event or holiday to holiday. Halloween is followed by Thanksgiving, and then comes Christmas, and so on. Lucky for me, Drew still hears the bells of Christmas and believes in all the magic of all the holidays. His childlike innocence and excitement, in many ways, is a silver lining.

Right after Valentine's Day, Drew begins to talk about the mischievous leprechaun and looks forward to his visit. I don't know what happens in other homes, but that leprechaun sneaks into our home on the eve of St. Patrick's Day and turns everything upside down looking for his gold. He flips sofa cushions, spills Lucky Charms, and leaves a trail of chocolate coins and treats as he dashes around our home. To this day Drew and our family cannot understand that despite setting traps to catch this leprechaun, he always gets away!

Drew is so excited that he can hardly sleep, and every St. Patrick's Day morning, we are awakened very early to Drew laughing and shouting, "That rotten leprechaun did it again, Mommy! He messed up your house and turned the milk green! How did that stinker get into our house? I told you he would!"

SCRIPTURE SUPPORT: PROVERBS 15:13 ESV

A glad heart makes a cheerful face, but by sorrow of heart the spirit is crushed.

Rainbow Reflection: Value Education

Schoolwork never came easy for Drew, but going to school was always easy. He demonstrates that there is so much value in education on a variety of levels. "I loved going to Kilgour Elementary because I felt happy and safe and all the teachers helped me."

SCRIPTURE SUPPORT: PROVERBS 4:13 ESV

Keep hold of instruction; do not let go; guard her, for she is your life.

MARCH 19

Rainbow Reflection: Be a Friend to Someone Today

It is so easy for individuals with exceptionalities to be a friend to one another and it is so beautiful to observe. The care, concern, and love they pour out are inspiring. Drew may be cognitively delayed, but his sensitivity is exceptional. Drew says, "Sometimes I feel down and then a friend cheers me up. When I see a friend who is sad, I try my best to cheer them up; I guess that is what it means to be friends."

SCRIPTURE SUPPORT: PSALMS 133:1 ESV

A Song of Ascents. Of David. Behold, how good and pleasant
it is when brothers dwell in unity.

Rainbow Reflection: Show Your Love and Gratitude

Drew gets very excited about his birthday on August 28th. When August arrives, the countdown begins.

"Mommy, only twenty-seven days until my birthday. Mommy, only twenty-six days until my birthday. Mommy, only twenty-five days until my birthday…" you get the picture. Some years I make a cake, and other years he requests a fancy cake from the bakery.

Last year was a bakery cake year, and Drew is friends with the pastry chef at the supermarket. The chef always makes time to chat with Drew and often gives him a cookie. While the chef always does a wonderful job with his pastries, he took such care with Drew's birthday cake.

At home, when it was time to sing "Happy Birthday," Drew was overjoyed with the cake, which was complete with Power Rangers on top!

The next time we were at the supermarket, Drew saw the pastry chef and unexpectedly ran behind the counter and gave him a gigantic hug while saying, "Thank you so much for my birthday cake; I loved it!"

While the hug took the pastry chef by surprise, he cheerfully returned the embrace and said, "Wow, I wish I always got that response! Drew, you encourage me to continue making each cake special; thank you."

SCRIPTURE SUPPORT: 1 CORINTHIANS 16:14 ESV

Let all that you do be done in love.

Rainbow Reflection:
Care for All

Individuals with exceptionalities often seem to have an elevated bond with and appreciation for pets. One friend with multiple exceptionalities shares, "Dogs take care of us, and we take care of them; we all have to take care of each other."

SCRIPTURE SUPPORT: GALATIANS 6:6 ESV

One who is taught the word must share all good things with the one who teaches.

Rainbow Reflection: Express Gratitude

Debbie and Doug are a married couple with exceptionalities. They always give thanks to God in all circumstances. Whether they need to fix a plumbing issue or they need to address a health concern, they always turn to God.

"We needed a new air conditioner and God answered our prayers, we were so happy."

SCRIPTURE SUPPORT: JOHN 15:7 ESV

If you abide in me, and my words abide in you,
ask whatever you wish, and it will be done for you.

Rainbow Reflection:
Show Commitment

Commitment is always important but when it is appreciated, it's even more rewarding. Maria, a friend with exceptionalities, looks with excitement to the end of her father's workday. "I love when Dad comes home from work. I wait for him because my dad plays with me every night even though he is tired."

SCRIPTURE SUPPORT: GALATIANS 6:9

And let us not grow weary of doing good,
for in due season we will reap, if we do not give up.

Rainbow Reflection:
Be Good to Others Even When It Is Hard

Frustration and anger are a part of the human experience, but guilt and self-loathing often occur when negative emotions are expressed.

Drew seems to live God's forgiveness to the fullest and simply tries to do better. He admits, "Sometimes my sisters make me angry, and God tells me not to yell at people; sometimes I still yell, but I try my best."

SCRIPTURE SUPPORT: 2 TIMOTHY 3:16-17 ESV

All Scripture is breathed out by God and profitable for teaching, for reproof, for correction and for training in righteousness, that the man of God may be competent, equipped for every good work.

Rainbow Reflection:
Push Beyond Your Comfort Level

Drew loves to dance and regularly attends a wonderful holiday party for children with exceptionalities. Leading up to the dance he perseverates about asking girls to dance, and one year, I overheard him talking to himself.

"I want to dance, but maybe no one will want to dance with me."

When the night of the dance arrived and despite feeling nervous, Drew pushed himself to ask a girl to dance. That was all it took, and for the rest of the evening, he danced the night away with one friend after another.

On the car ride home, as he was looking out the window he said, "Mommy, I was feeling kind of shy, but I asked the girl to dance and she said yes; it was so much fun."

Drew reminded me the importance of pushing beyond your comfort level.

SCRIPTURE SUPPORT: MATTHEW 18:3 ESV

And he said, "Truly, I say to you, unless you turn and become like children, you will never enter the kingdom of heaven."

Rainbow Reflection:
Take Time Daily to Pray,
Mediate, or Reflect

Drew seems to physically and spiritually benefit from prayer. He says, "I feel so happy and calm when I talk to God."

SCRIPTURE SUPPORT: PSALMS 19:14 ESV

Let the words of my mouth and the mediation of my heart be acceptable
in your sight, O Lord my rock and my redeemer

Rainbow Reflection: Remember That Love Is Everything

Drew has one special friend that he has known since his grade school years. Their friendship and affection are so pure and sincere.

She earnestly expressed, "If I could wish for one thing, it would be to marry Andrew."

SCRIPTURE SUPPORT: GENESIS 2:18 ESV

Then the Lord God said, "It is not good that the man should be alone,
I will make him a helper fit for him."

Rainbow Reflection:
Achieve Something Each Day

While many people downplay a personal victory, individuals with exceptionalities often celebrate their success.

Drew says, "I am proud when I set a goal and do it." Drew and his friends seem to comfortably celebrate their personal success and the achievements of others.

SCRIPTURE SUPPORT: PHILIPPIANS 4:13 ESV

I can do all things through him who strengthens me.

Rainbow Reflection: Don't Be Afraid to Ask for Help

Children with exceptionalities remind me that it is okay to be vulnerable and to ask for help. Often the exchange is mutually beneficial because in helping others, we help ourselves.

A friend with dwarfism says, "If I'm struggling, I call someone."

SCRIPTURE SUPPORT: ROMANS 12:5 ESV

So we, though many, are one body in Christ and
individually members one of another.

Rainbow Reflection:
Never Give Up

Why is it that children with exceptionalities just seem to get it? Often people berate themselves when a mistake is made or end up frustrated, disappointed, and discouraged. Our good friend John says, "Sometimes you need a second chance, people to cheer you on, and then you try to do better."

SCRIPTURE SUPPORT: PHILIPPIANS 4:12-13 ESV

I know how to be brought low, and I know how to abound. In any and every circumstance, I have learned the secret of facing plenty and hunger, abundance and need. I can do all things through him who strengthens me.

Rainbow Reflection:
Find Your Safe Place and Visit Often

A classmate with Down syndrome recognized the importance of going where you feel welcome.

She said, "In church I feel comfortable."

SCRIPTURE SUPPORT: 1 CORINTHIANS 14:26 ESV

What then, brothers? When you come together, each one has a hymn, a lesson, a revelation, a tongue, or an interpretation. Let all things be done for building up.

Rainbow Reflection: Recognize God's Unyielding Love for Us

Easter season can be difficult for Drew. He struggles greatly with the cruelty that Jesus endured for us. He often cries and even calls out, "Why were they so mean to Jesus, Mommy?"

How do you answer a child with such a pure heart to help him understand the ultimate sacrifice God gave to the world in his only son? I just reply, "Because he loves us so much."

SCRIPTURE SUPPORT: JOHN 15:12 ESV

This is my commandment, that you love one another as I have loved you.

APRIL 2

Rainbow Reflection: Question Cruelty

Easter is a time of sorrow and joy. At church I look over at Drew who is silently looking up at the cross with tears running down his face. Through his tears and broken heart, he asks, "Why did they have to nail him to the cross?"

SCRIPTURE SUPPORT: PROVERBS 11:17 ESV

A man who is kind benefits himself, but a cruel man hurts himself.

Rainbow Reflection: Rejoice

Drew is so grateful on Easter morning and with folded hands and closed eyes he prays,

"Thank you, God, today our Jesus is off that cross."

SCRIPTURE SUPPORT: ROMANS 6:23 ESV

For the wages of sin is death, but the free gift of God
is eternal life in Christ Jesus our Lord.

APRIL 4

Rainbow Reflection: Remember to Laugh Today

The family can always count on Grandpa to make us laugh, and his sense of humor reminds us of the importance of fun. Through giggles, Drew says, "Grandpa is funny, and he makes silly nicknames for me and all of my cousins."

SCRIPTURE SUPPORT: GENESIS 21:6

"God has made laughter for me; everyone who hears will laugh over me."

Rainbow Reflection:
Believe in Things You Can't Always See

At age twenty-three, Drew says with such confusion, "I have no idea how that Easter Bunny hops into our house when all the doors were locked!" His sense of wonder is refreshing and magical.

SCRIPTURE SUPPORT: MARK 10:27 ESV

Jesus looked at them and said, "With man it is impossible, but not with God. For all things are possible with God."

Rainbow Reflection:
Trust That Everything Will Work Out

Oh, to be so lighthearted and carefree. Each day I strive to be more like Drew and so many of his friends who seem to approach life with such confidence that all will be okay.

Drew reminds me, "Don't worry, Mommy, because worrying is not a good thing to do."

SCRIPTURE SUPPORT: 2 THESSALONIANS 3:16 ESV

Now may the Lord of peace himself give you peace at all times in every way.
The Lord be with you all.

Rainbow Reflection: Believe Anything Is Possible

Dancing with his whole heart in his "original and unique way," Drew says, "Maybe I could get on *America's Got Talent* with my dancing. When I win, it will be a dream come true because I will use the money to buy Bengals season tickets real close to the field!"

SCRIPTURE SUPPORT: ROMANS 15:13 ESV

May the God of hope fill you with all joy and peace in believing. So that by the power of thy Holy Spirit you may abound in hope.

Rainbow Reflection: Let Someone Know How Important They Are to You

I've noticed that when it comes to emotions and feelings, many of us think before we speak and then never speak. However, saying what you feel seems to come so easy to many people with exceptionalities. Drew openly expresses, "I don't like it when you go on the plane because I miss you and sometimes it makes me sad."

SCRIPTURE SUPPORT: GENESIS 31:49

And Mizpah, for he said, "The Lord watch between you and me, when we are out of one another's sight."

Rainbow Reflection: Express Appreciation

Drew and I finish up at the cell phone store and Drew stops at the door, looks out across the crowded store, and gives the sales associate a thumbs up, saying loudly, "Thank you for helping my mommy."

He then ran over and gave him a "You're Special" rainbow card. The sales associate replies, "Wow, this job can sometimes feel a bit thankless and stressful; that was great to hear today."

Years later that card is still proudly displayed in the store.

SCRIPTURE SUPPORT: COLOSSIANS 3:15 ESV

And let the peace of Christ rule in your hearts,
to which indeed you were called in one body. And be thankful.

APRIL 10

Rainbow Reflection: Pray Often and Together

Drew does not consider prayer a burden. He views it as a conversation and often a shared activity.

He admits, "One of my favorite things about going to Grandma and Grandpa's house is that we always pray together."

SCRIPTURE SUPPORT: MATTHEW 18:20

For where two or three are gathered in my name, there am I among them.

Rainbow Reflection: Look for the Good in Others

It is so easy to see our faults, mistakes, disappointments, regrets, but Drew and so many of his friends with exceptionalities seem to see the best in others. Drew often says, "I see your angel wings, Mommy."

On my worst days, Drew in his special way, and through his unique perspective, always manages to see the best in me. I am not deserving but I am grateful.

SCRIPTURE SUPPORT: HEBREWS 2:12 ESV

Saying, "I will tell of your name to my brothers;
in the midst of the congregation I will sing your praise."

APRIL 12

Rainbow Reflection: Appreciate Right Where You Are and Enjoy the Moment

In Pee Wee Football, Drew goes to every practice and gives it his all but doesn't get any "real" playing time. The highlight for him is on game day when the announcer introduces each player and it is finally his turn.

"No. 4, Slamming Andrew Leurck!"

Drew runs across the field with a big smile, waving crazily and yelling, "Hi Mommy, hi Daddy!"

He is happy and content to be part of the team and his enthusiasm is contagious. He quite possibly gets the loudest cheers from the crowd.

SCRIPTURE SUPPORT: PHILIPPIANS 4:4 ESV

Rejoice in the Lord always; again, I will say, Rejoice.

Rainbow Reflection: Honor Someone's Request Today

I've learned that small gestures have great impact. Still to this day and at age twenty-three, Drew still finds comfort in bedtime routines and often asks, "Will you come and tuck me in, Mommy?"

SCRIPTURE SUPPORT: PSALMS 119:76 ESV

Let your steadfast love comfort me according to your promise to your servant.

APRIL 14

Rainbow Reflection: Cherish Friendship

After a disappointing cut from a sports team, a friend with Asperger syndrome said, "Sometimes life is hard, but my friends always make me feel better. I think having friends is a good thing to have." The love and caring that is observed among people with exceptionalities is inspiring.

SCRIPTURE SUPPORT: PROVERBS 27:9 ESV

Oil and perfume make the heart glad, and the sweetness
of a friend comes from his earnest counsel.

Rainbow Reflection: Marvel at How Much God Loves You

Drew confidently states, "A rainbow is the sign of God's love."

"How do you know this, Drew? Who told you this?"

"Mommy, sometimes when I sleep at night, I sit on Jesus's lap and he tells me things."

SCRIPTURE SUPPORT: EZEKIEL 1:28 ESV

Like the appearance of the bow that is in the cloud on a day of rain, so was the appearance of the brightness all around. Such was the appearance of the likeness of the glory of the Lord. And when I saw it, I fell on my face, and I heard the voice of one speaking.

Rainbow Reflection: Find Comfort in Being a Child of God

It is remarkable how some very philosophical insights come so easily to so many people with exceptionalities. Their matter-of-fact acceptance to very difficult and provocative thoughts is inspiring. A wheelchair-bound individual with limited movement does not complain. He says, "I stay positive because I know that I was created by God."

SCRIPTURE SUPPORT: 1 PETER 1:3 ESV

Blessed be the God and Father of our Lord Jesus Christ! According to his great mercy, he has caused us to be born again to a living hope through the resurrection of Jesus Christ from the dead.

Rainbow Reflection:
Know When It Is Time to Let Go

Our dear Goldendoodle Maggie is fifteen, and she is not well. She struggles to walk and has trouble breathing. It seems everyone in the family recognizes it is time, but I cannot seem to let my girl go. She has been my constant companion, a confidante, a mother's helper, and a most loyal friend.

Drew and Maggie are also very tight, and I worry about the impact on him. Recently, I asked Drew his opinion and was surprised with his response which he so confidently shared.

"Mommy, it is time for Maggie to go to heaven. When she gets there, she can run and play with Grandma's doggie Opie, and our bunnies, Blossom and Daisy. Mommy, when we get to heaven, she will be right there waiting for us."

God Bless Maggie Leurck October 21, 2004 - May 9, 2020

SCRIPTURE SUPPORT: GENESIS 1:25

And God made the beasts of the earth according to their kinds and the livestock according to their kinds, and everything that creeps on the ground according to its kind. And God saw that it was good.

Rainbow Reflection:
Keep Moving Forward

The perspective of one of Drew's friends with exceptionalities is remarkable in its simplicity. "We all get sad sometimes and it is normal, but you just can't stay sad for too long."

SCRIPTURE SUPPORT: PSALMS 18:2 ESV

The Lord is my rock and my fortress and my deliverer, my God, my rock, in whom I take refuge, my shield, and the horn of my salvation, my stronghold.

Rainbow Reflection:
Stay the Course

The outlook of our friend John who has Williams syndrome is so profoundly philosophical and motivating. "You cannot let anything negative define you. Life might be hard but it is so worth it at the end of the day."

SCRIPTURE SUPPORT: 2 THESSALONIANS 3:13

As for you, brothers, do not grow weary in doing good.

Rainbow Reflection: Take Time to Relax

L ife is busy, and Drew often reminds me to take time for fun, relaxation, and entertainment. He says, "Thank you, Mommy, for taking me to the game; I just love the Reds and going to the stadium."

SCRIPTURE SUPPORT: 1 CORINTHIANS 10:31

So, whether you eat or drink, or whatever you do, do all to the glory of God.

APRIL 21

Rainbow Reflection:
Value Friendship

L inda has been a mentor to Drew for many years. We consider her part of our family, and she is very special to Drew. They see each other every week and go out into the community to work on social and life skills. They are the best of buddies and her loyalty and commitment to Drew are priceless.

"Ms. Linda is always there for me; she is one of my best friends."

SCRIPTURE SUPPORT: 1 PETER 3:15 ESV

But in your hearts honor Christ the Lord as holy, always being prepared to make a defense to anyone who asks you for a reason for the hope that is in you; yet do it with gentleness and respect.

APRIL 22

Rainbow Reflection: Shepherd One Another

Drew is most aware of his herd and never leaves anyone behind. When in a group, he is always the shepherd. He comments, "We are walking too fast, and Grandma is falling behind; we have to wait."

SCRIPTURE SUPPORT: PROVERBS 27:23 ESV

Know well the condition of your flocks, and give attention to your herds

Rainbow Reflection:
Be a Hero to Someone

Drew eats too fast and takes big bites. We still cut up his food for him but on a family vacation and in the chaos of a big extended family dinner, Drew began eating his chicken breast too quickly. The dining room was bustling with activity when Alexandra screamed, "Drew is choking!"

The next moments were some of the scariest of my life as several unsuccessful attempts were made to dislodge the chicken. Drew was not making any sound and time was of the essence when Uncle Greg, Drew's godfather stepped in and performed the Heimlich.

He was successful, and Drew's godfather also became his guardian angel. Drew knew I was so rattled and kept repeating, "I'm sorry it scared you when I choked, Mommy, but Uncle Greg, my godfather, fixed it."

SCRIPTURE SUPPORT: GALATIANS 6:2 ESV

Bear one another's burdens, and so fulfill the law of Christ.

Rainbow Reflection:
Never Take Things for Granted

So often the simple things in life are taken for granted, but that is rarely the case for Drew. I'm in awe of how individuals with exceptionalities have such perspective. Drew comments, "It makes me sad that some people don't have food or a warm home."

SCRIPTURE SUPPORT: PHILIPPIANS 4:19

And my god will supply every need of yours
according to his riches in glory in Christ Jesus.

Rainbow Reflection: Think Big

Drew's confidence never ceases to amaze me. With just one tenth of his assurance, we could move mountains. With 100% certainty, Drew exclaims, "I'm pretty good at basketball; maybe I should play with LeBron."

SCRIPTURE SUPPORT: MATTHEW 25:15 ESV

To one he gave five talents. To another two., to another one,
to each according to his ability. Then he went away.

Rainbow Reflection:
Seek to Comfort Others in
Difficult Times

The value of friendship is apparent to all humans, but I've noticed that individuals with exceptionalities seem to pay very close attention and regularly check in on one another. "My friends cheer me up when I feel sad."

SCRIPTURE SUPPORT: ECCLESIASTES 3:12 ESV

I perceived that there is nothing better for them to be joyful
and to do good as long as they live.

Rainbow Reflection: Speak Gratitude

As a result of text and email, handwritten thank you notes are becoming a thing of the past, but Drew seems to delight in writing them. If anyone does something kind for him or gives him a gift, without prompting, Drew will write a note. He finds joy in expressing gratitude.

SCRIPTURE SUPPORT: COLOSSIANS 3:17 ESV

And whatever you do, in word or deed, do everything in the name of the Lord Jesus giving thanks to God the Father through him.

Rainbow Reflection:
Put One Foot in Front of the Other

Individuals with exceptionalities remind me to never give up. A classmate with Down syndrome says, "I wanted the Chargers to win; I bet they are sad. But someone must win, and someone must lose, so they can't give up. I think they will win the next game!"

SCRIPTURE SUPPORT: JAMES 1:12 ESV

Blessed is the man who remains steadfast under trial,
for when he has stood the test, he will receive the crown of life,
which God has promised to those who love him.

APRIL 29

Rainbow Reflection: Cherish All God's Creatures

"It makes me sad that some animals are endangered; Mommy, how can we help them?" Drew asks.

SCRIPTURE SUPPORT: JOB 12:7-10 ESV

But ask the beasts, and they will teach you; the birds of the heavens, and they will tell you; or the bushes of the earth, and they will teach you; and the fish of the sea will declare to you, Who among all these does not know that the hand of the Lord has done this? In his hand is the life of every living thing and the breath of all mankind.

Rainbow Reflection:
Appreciate the Little Joys in Life

The Oaks is the horse race that occurs the day before the Kentucky Derby. It is filled with fanfare and pageantry and is one of Drew's favorite events.

One year, Drew and his father met a group of men with a horse in the actual Oaks race. Leading up to the race, Drew and these men had a great time visiting and they treated Drew to several pops. In Drew's world, the day could not get any better.

It was time for the owner's horse to race and they told Drew that if their horse won, he was invited to come down to the Winner's Circle with them.

The race began, and ladies in beautiful hats and men in bow ties cheered on their favorite filly. The owner's horse won, and Drew got to go down to the Winner's Circle at Churchill Downs, a once in a lifetime experience!

When I finally got to talk to Drew, I could not wait to hear all the details, but he didn't tell me about the winning race, and he didn't tell me about the Winner's Circle.

With such excitement in his voice, as if he couldn't believe his luck, he said,

"Mommy, you won't believe it, they bought me pops all day long."

It's the little things!

KATHERINE THOMAS LEURCK

SCRIPTURE SUPPORT: PSALMS 118:24 ESV

This is the day that the Lord has made; let us rejoice and be glad in it.

MAY 1

Rainbow Reflection: Once in a While, Get Gussied Up and Go Out

Drew reminds me when you look good, you feel good. His excitement is apparent as he prepares for the "Run for the Roses." He says, "I feel handsome when I put on my bow tie and go to the Kentucky Derby."

SCRIPTURE SUPPORT: 2 TIMOTHY 2:15 ESV

Do your best to present yourself to God as one approved, a worker who has no need to be ashamed, rightly handling the word of truth.

Rainbow Reflection:
Love Yourself as God Loves You

Drew sees beauty at all ages, and he is generous with his compliments. He tells his grandma, "You are pretty, Grandma Bev."

Grandma replies, "Thank you, Drew, and there was a day when that was true."

"No, Grandma, don't say that. You are still pretty," Drew replies.

SCRIPTURE SUPPORT: 1 CORINTHIANS 6:20 ESV

For you were bought with a price. So, glorify God in your body.

MAY 3

Rainbow Reflection:
Respect All Ages and Stages

I have no idea how young individuals with exceptionalities can be so insightful at their tender ages, but they seem to understand so much.

"It doesn't matter if young or old, you still want to laugh," says a friend with cerebral palsy.

SCRIPTURE SUPPORT: PROVERBS 20:29 ESV

The glory of young men is their strength,
but the splendor of old men is their gray hair.

MAY 4

Rainbow Reflection: Surround Yourself with People Who Make You Better

So often people try to work for approval or to "win people over." I've noticed that individuals with exceptionalities seek healthy and inviting companionship.

"I want to hang out with my family and friends because they make me feel comfortable," replied a friend with hearing loss when asked about weekend plans.

SCRIPTURE SUPPORT: PROVERBS 27:17

Iron sharpens iron, and one man sharpens another.

MAY 5

Rainbow Reflection:
Find Comfort in Prayer

A child with Down syndrome reminds me the importance of quiet time and prayer. "At night, I talk to God and I feel at peace."

SCRIPTURE SUPPORT: 1 THESSALONIANS 5:17 ESV

Pray without ceasing

Rainbow Reflection: Appreciate Community

Being a part of community is an essential human element for connection and inclusion.

"I want to go to church because I see Jesus and other people; it's kind of nice at church."

SCRIPTURE SUPPORT: 1 JOHN 1:7 ESV

But if we walk in the light, as he is in the light, we have fellowship with one another, and the blood of Jesus his Son cleanses us from all sin.

Rainbow Reflection:
Talk to God About Everything

Debbie and Doug are a married couple with exceptionalities and they always remember to turn to God with all problems, both big and little. They understand that with God all things are possible.

"Our air conditioner went out, and we live on the 3rd floor, so it gets really hot. I prayed and prayed for a new air conditioner. Guess what? We got one, and the salesman even gave us half off!"

SCRIPTURE SUPPORT: MATTHEW 7:7

"Ask, and it will be given to you; seek, and you will find;
knock, and it will be opened to you.

Rainbow Reflection:
See Your Gifts and the Gifts in Others

Many of us are inclined to see faults, especially within ourselves. I have often marveled at the confidence and gratitude of the individuals with exceptionalities. One child with autism shared, "If I could talk to Jesus, I would thank him for making me so great."

Amen!

SCRIPTURE SUPPORT: JEREMIAH 1:5 ESV

"Before I formed you in the womb, I knew you, and before you were born, I consecrated you; I appointed you a prophet to the nations."

Rainbow Reflection:
Take Care of One Another

Drew always puts people first and often their needs before his. He reminds me to always be thoughtful and caring.

For being "delayed," Drew certainly understands the care we give him and the importance of caring for others.

He sweetly says, "Mommy, thank you for taking care of me. Don't worry about when you get old, because I'll take care of you. I guess we take care of each other."

SCRIPTURE SUPPORT: 1 PETER 3:8 ESV

Finally, all of you, have unity of mind, sympathy, brotherly love, a tender heart, and a humble mind.

MAY 10

Rainbow Reflection: Be Boundless in Your Love

I'm often reminded by Drew to never miss an opportunity to tell someone how much you love them.

"Sissy, I love you to the world and back," says Drew.

"I love you to heaven and back--beat that, Mommy!" Drew calls from his bedroom.

"I'm glad I told Grandpa how much I loved him before he went to heaven," Drew comments at Grandpa's funeral.

SCRIPTURE SUPPORT: 1 PETER 4:8 ESV

Above all, keep loving one another earnestly, since love covers a multitude of sins. Show hospitality to one another without grumbling. As each has received a gift, use it to serve one another, as good steward of God's varied grace.

Rainbow Reflection:
Find Joy in Giving

It doesn't have to take a lot of money to share joy. I've witnessed again and again how a small card with a simple rainbow can become a priceless gift. Drew comments, "Some people don't have presents and that makes me very sad; that is why I like to pass out rainbows, because the rainbows make people happy."

SCRIPTURE SUPPORT: CORINTHIANS 9:7 ESV

Each one must give as he has decided in his heart, not reluctantly or under compulsion, for God loves a cheerful giver.

Rainbow Reflection: Keep Romance Alive

Although Drew will probably never get his driver's license, his heart is filled with the romance of going on a date and driving his own car someday. He thoughtfully dreams, "When I grow up and go on dates, I will pick my date up in a red Fiat convertible, and I think she will feel very special."

SCRIPTURE SUPPORT: PROVERBS 5:18-19 ESV

Let your fountain be blessed, and rejoice in the wife of your youth,
a lovely deer, a graceful doe.

Rainbow Reflection:
Find Value in Hard Work

"Sometimes I don't feel like doing chores, but I do them because my parents ask me, and when I'm done, I feel proud." Drew gets it.

SCRIPTURE SUPPORT: PROVERBS 13:4 ESV

The soul of the sluggard craves and gets nothing,
while the soul of the diligent is richly supplied.

Rainbow Reflection:
Be a Trailblazer

Alaina, who has dwarfism, embraces life and all its challenges with positive energy. She proudly exclaims, "I am in two choirs, I am a cheerleader, and I love school. I like to show others that people who are different can do anything that anyone else can do."

SCRIPTURE SUPPORT: MATTHEW 19:26 ESV

But Jesus looked at them and said, "With man this is impossible, but with God all things are possible."

Rainbow Reflection:
Strive to Accept Change as It Is
Inevitable

Drew's sister will be starting college next fall, and this has made Drew very distraught. It will be a big shift and change to the household dynamics. With no warning and on multiple occasions, Drew will come to me in tears and say, "I'm so sad Sissy has to go away to college; I'm going to miss her."

I explain that it is her time to spread her wings and fly and he replies, "Mom, she is not a bird and cannot fly, and I want her to stay right here with us."

SCRIPTURE SUPPORT: ECCLESIASTES 3:1 ESV

For everything there is a season, and a time for every matter under heaven.

Rainbow Reflection: Think Happy Thoughts

A brilliant reminder from a friend with exceptionalities: "I think you should not be sad for too long; if you stay sad for too long, you just feel worse. It is best to go and do something fun and to smile."

SCRIPTURE SUPPORT: PSALM 28:7 ESV

The Lord is my strength and my shield; in him my heart trusts, and I am helped; my heart exults, and with my song I give thanks to him.

Rainbow Reflection:
Stay in Touch

People with exceptionalities seem to understand the importance of connecting.

At a recent Drew's Rainbows gathering I overheard a child with cerebal palsy share, "I like visiting with friends I haven't seen in a while because I can hang out and catch up."

SCRIPTURE SUPPORT: ROMANS 12:5 ESV

So, we, through many, are one body in Christ,
and individually members one of another.

Rainbow Reflection: Remember You Are a Creation of the Most High God

Unlike many of us who often doubt our value, Drew always recognizes his gifts. Upon graduation he comments,

"I think I'm pretty smart, because God made me."

SCRIPTURE SUPPORT: 2 CORINTHIANS 3:5

Not that we are sufficient in ourselves to claim anything as coming from us, but our sufficiency is from God.

Rainbow Reflection:
Take Time to Rest

D rew intuitively respects and listens to his body. When he is tired, it is as if a light switch goes off. Yawning, he exclaims, "I'm so tired and I think I hit a wall so, I'm going to hit the hay."

SCRIPTURE SUPPORT: PSALMS 4:8 ESV

In peace I will both lie down and sleep; for you alone,
O Lord, make me dwell in safety.

Rainbow Reflection: Be Inclusive

Individuals with exceptionalities are often excluded, but they inherently seem to understand the importance of including others. Drew shares, "I like to play with everyone because it makes them smile."

SCRIPTURE SUPPORT: ROMANS 15:7 ESV

Therefore welcome one another as Christ has welcomed you, for the glory of God.

Rainbow Reflection: Compliment Others

Passing out compliments seems to come naturally to individuals with exceptionalities. "When I see a pretty girl, I want to tell her that she looks beautiful. I think it makes people happy when I give them compliments," Drew proudly states.

SCRIPTURE SUPPORT: ROMANS 15:2 ESV

Let each of us please his neighbor for his good, to build him up.

Rainbow Reflection:
Put Empathy into Action

After an exciting downtown visit during the holidays, Drew ponders the day. I assume he is contemplating the decorations, the bigger than life Christmas tree, but his thoughts are of others. "It makes me sad when people don't have food or a home, and I want to help."

SCRIPTURE SUPPORT: PROVERBS 22:9 ESV

Whoever has a bountiful eye will be blessed, for he shares his bread with the poor.

Rainbow Reflection: Give Thanks and Praise

Doug has exceptionalities and his confidence and faith in eternal salvation inspires. "If I could talk to Jesus, I would thank him for helping me get to heaven."

SCRIPTURE SUPPORT: ACTS 16:31 ESV

And they said, "Believe in the Lord Jesus,
and you will be saved, you and your household."

MAY 24

———

Rainbow Reflection:
Volunteer Your Time and Talent

After participating in a volunteer event, a friend with Down syndrome spoke so eloquently about the day. "When we helped the people, it made my heart feel good. It is right to help others."

SCRIPTURE SUPPORT: LUKE 3:10-11 ESV

And the crowds asked him, "What then shall we do?" And he answered them, "Whoever has two tunics to share with him who has none, and whoever has food is to do likewise."

Rainbow Reflection:
Have a Sense of Humor

"**M**y sisters are important to me because we have fun and some-times, I tickle them; they don't like it, but that kind of makes me laugh." Drew understands the importance of humor and good clean fun.

SCRIPTURE SUPPORT: PROVERBS 19:11 ES

Good sense makes one slow to anger, and it is his glory to overlook an offense.

Rainbow Reflection:
Visualize Yourself Accomplishing Big Things

So often it is human nature to doubt oneself:

"I probably won't get the job."

"I don't think I'll ever meet Mr. Right."

"I doubt we will ever get ahead financially."

"I'd love to take that dream trip, but that'll never happen."

Individuals with exceptionalities often imagine that anything is possible. With little thought to the **impossibility**, I have overheard the following comments with complete confidence from individuals with exceptionalities.

"I could see myself being on *Dancing with the Stars*, and I'd probably win."

"I could see myself as a famous artist."

"One day, I think I will be a pro athlete."

"I can't wait to play on the Bengals with Joe Burrow."

SCRIPTURE SUPPORT: MARK 9:23

And Jesus said to him, "If you can! All things are possible for one who believes."

Rainbow Reflection:
Be Open to New Experiences

Doug, who is an individual with exceptionalities, loves Elvis. On a regular basis, he dons his Elvis costume and takes his impersonation show on the road. He volunteers to visit retirement communities to entertain the residents.

In addition to performing, he takes his hard-earned paycheck from his job at a fast food restaurant, and purchases gifts and treats to pass out to his "fans." Doug orchestrated this plan all on his own and said, "Why not? You should always try new things."

SCRIPTURE SUPPORT: 1 PETER 4:10 ESV

As each has received a gift. Use it to serve one another,
as good stewards of God's varied grace.

Rainbow Reflection:
Imagine Possibilities

Drew always dreams big. He states, "I might marry Dakota, Ellen, Maria, Olivia, or Christine; I'm just not sure which one it will be yet, but it will probably be one of them."

The way he imagines possibilities makes me smile.

SCRIPTURE SUPPORT: ROMANS 8:25 ESV

But if we hope for what we do not see, we wait for it with patience.

Rainbow Reflection: Find Joy in the Little Things

McDonalds is a treat , and when we road trip to the beach, we always begin the trip with a "car picnic," which is McDonalds for breakfast. Ironically, when I asked Drew what he loves most about going to the beach, it isn't the ocean, the sunsets, the seashells or the boats. Drew replied, "My favorite is when we get McDonalds for breakfast."

SCRIPTURE SUPPORT: PROVERBS 15:3 ESV

The eyes of the Lord are in every place, keeping watch on the evil and the good.

Rainbow Reflection: Recognize the Gifts that Others Offer to Us

A child with ADHD shares, "I like seeing older people because they are always nice to me, and they take time to talk to me a lot."

SCRIPTURE SUPPORT: ROMANS 12 6-8 ESV

Having gifts that differ according to the grace given to us, let us use them; if prophecy, in proportion to our faith; if service, in our serving; the one who teaches, in his teaching; the one who exhorts, in his exhortation; the one who contributes, in generosity; the one who leads, with zeal; the one who does acts of mercy, with cheerfulness.

Rainbow Reflection:
Pray for Our Service Men and Women

Drew's Great Grandpa Gene was a paratrooper in World War II and his Grandpa Ron was a Marine. Soldiers are heroes to Drew.

At the Normandy memorial in France, Drew placed his rainbow cards at soldiers' graves.

Without prompting, he knelt, closed his eyes and prayed, "Dear Jesus, please keep our soldiers safe."

SCRIPTURE SUPPORT: ROMANS 13:4 ESV

For he is God's servant for your good. But if you do wrong, be afraid, for he does not bear the sword in vain. For he is the servant of the God, an avenger who carries out God's wrath on the wrongdoer.

JUNE 1

Rainbow Reflection: Talk Through Problems

It is a powerful moment when anyone uses words instead of force. It was especially rewarding to hear a child on the Autism spectrum advocate for himself and express, "It frustrates me when people tease me, so I use my words to tell them to quit."

SCRIPTURE SUPPORT: JAMES 1:19 ESV

Know this, my beloved brothers; let every person be quick to hear, slow to speak, slow to anger.

Rainbow Reflection:
Trust in God

Drew is a child of God and trusts his Father wholeheartedly.

Drew says, "If I could talk to Jesus, I'd probably tell him, 'I'll follow you wherever you go.'"

SCRIPTURE SUPPORT: JOHN 8:12 ESV

Again, Jesus spoke to them, saying, "I am the light of the world. Whoever follows me will not walk in darkness but will have the light of life."

JUNE 3

Rainbow Reflection:
See God in Everyone

Individuals with exceptionalities are often extremely observant.

Drew seems to notice the feelings and energy of others. He shares, "When I see someone who is lonely, it makes me sad, and I want to give them a rainbow because they are special to me."

SCRIPTURE SUPPORT: PSALMS 139:14

I praise you, for I am fearfully and wonderfully made. Wonderful are your works; my soul knows it very well.

Rainbow Reflection: Appreciate Community

Appreciation comes naturally to many individuals with exceptionalities. Some show it through their eyes, others show it with affection, many share a smile, some use their words.

One friend with dwarfism said, "Around my teachers, I feel good, and they are very helpful."

SCRIPTURE SUPPORT: PROVERBS 22:6

Train up a child in the way he should go; even when he is old,
he will not depart from it.

JUNE 5

Rainbow Reflection: Be Caring

Empathy seems to be a natural attribute to many children with exceptionalities.

A child with ADHD expressed it sweetly when he said, "When my sister is sick, I tell her to sip on 7-up, I hold her hand, and I try to be extra nice."

SCRIPTURE SUPPORT: 2 TIMOTHY 3:17 ESV

That the man of God may be competent, equipped for every good work.

Rainbow Reflection: Expect Miracles

Sometimes things just magically happen for Drew. While he is challenged, as I look back on his life, I realize his exceptionalities often enable many abilities.

While filming the grass roots short documentary titled *Drew Gets It,* in New York City, a small miracle occurred.

We are filming at Grand Central Station and things are going well. Drew is busy passing out his rainbow cards with great reception. Busy New Yorkers, tourists, Wall Street types and families, meet Drew with a smile, a thank you, and often a hug. It is beautiful to witness.

As we are filming, we are suddenly interrupted by an authoritative and stern-looking security guard who asks, "What are you doing?"

We explain that we are filming a short documentary about the message of love and how Drew likes to remind everyone they're special by passing out his simple rainbow drawing.

The security guard responds, "That's cool, but do you have a permit?" He goes on to say, "Professional filming in Grand Central Station requires a badge and permit and it takes time to acquire. How long will you be filming the documentary?"

In disbelief, I quietly reply, "We flew in from Cincinnati with a small crew and have only today."

The security guard looks out across the busy crowd and spots Drew, who is oblivious to our conversation and is talking, making friends, taking pictures, and passing out his rainbow cards.

"Hold on and wait here," he says.

He goes off and hovers in a corner of the station to make a call. A few minutes later he returns, points to me and says, "Mom, get moving. You are going to go to our main office and explain what you are doing. I cannot make any promises, but I did tell the office you were coming."

I waste no time and traverse the gigantic train station, up stairways, through tunnels, down halls, and finally up an elevator that opens to a serious and intimidating gatekeeper.

"What do you need?" she flatly asks.

I begin to explain that the security guard called ahead but before I can finish, she interrupts, "Hold on."

With her back to me, she has a phone conversation as I nervously await. When she turns around, I notice a shift in her disposition.

She says, "I don't know what you are up to, but it must be special, because I have been informed to give you an all-access day pass."

I can hardly believe my ears, but I quickly thank her and give her a "You're Special" rainbow card. She reads it, cracks a smile, and says, "Get out of here and put that pass to good use!"

I rush back to share the great news that we are officially back in action.

After a short time, a professional and well-dressed man thanks Drew for the rainbow and says, "I will keep this in my wallet; thank you." He turns to me and asks, "By the way, how did you get the permit to film in Grand Central station?"

I explain the story and he says in disbelief, "I'll be damned. I've spent a year and over $100,000 trying to film a commercial here, only to be rejected." He gives Drew a high five and says, "Little man, you are the one who is special."

About that time, the security guard who had helped us walks up and says, "I'm so glad to see that things worked out, and God Bless."

It was only at that moment I noticed the security guard's name on his badge:

Juan Baptiste (John the Baptist)

SCRIPTURE SUPPORT: ROMANS 8:31 ESV

What then shall we say to these things? If God is for us, who can be against us?

Rainbow Reflection:
Have Heroes

The impact of important people is not lost on individuals with exceptionalities. Drew loves seeing his coaches and teammates.

He comments, "When I see Coach Howie and Max, I am so happy because they helped me in football."

SCRIPTURE SUPPORT: MATTHEW 7:12 ESV

"So, whatever you wish that others would do to you, do also to them, for this is the Law and the Prophets."

JUNE 8

Rainbow Reflection:
Remember That Love Is Always the Answer

It is important to limit the news Drew watches because the violence and headlines often upset him.

He cannot understand why the world struggles to embrace the simple notion of loving one another.

He says, "God tells us we should all love one another, but people just don't want to listen."

SCRIPTURE SUPPORT: ROMANS 13:8

Owe no one anything, except to love each other,
for the one who loves another has fulfilled the law.

JUNE 9

Rainbow Reflection: Slow Down

"I don't like when we are so busy, because then we can't play our card games." Such simple words from a child with a cognition delay that elevates the importance of time.

SCRIPTURE SUPPORT: EPHESIANS 5:15-17 ESV

Look carefully then how you walk, not as unwise but as wise, making the best use of the time, because the days are evil. Therefore, do not be foolish, but understand what the will of the Lord is.

JUNE 10

Rainbow Reflection: Keep Memories Alive

"Mommy told me that some say cardinals are like angels from heaven. So, when I see a cardinal, I think of Patricia and Grandpa." Drew's comments help to keep the memories alive.

SCRIPTURE SUPPORT: PSALMS 91:11 ESV

For he will command his angels concerning you to guard you in all your ways.

Rainbow Reflection: Always Strive for Patience

"**M**y puppy sometimes plays too rough , and I tell her, no biting, but I have to be patient because she is still learning."

Drew's comment is an unintentional and subtle reminder to be patient with all who are still learning.

SCRIPTURE SUPPORT: ROMANS 2:7 ESV

To those who by patience in well-doing seek for glory and honor and immortality, he will give eternal life.

JUNE 12

Rainbow Reflection: Be Civil with Others

At a small gathering of individuals with exceptionalities, it was nice to hear one child remind the group, "Yelling hurts my ears; it is not nice to yell."

SCRIPTURE SUPPORT: EXODUS 14:14 ESV

The Lord will fight for you, and you have only to be silent.

JUNE 13

Rainbow Reflection:
Strive for Peace

"I wish God would help people to quit fighting; they should learn to just get along and have fun like me and my friend Brian." Drew expresses so simply the ease between him and his friend Brian who have never shared a cross word.

SCRIPTURE SUPPORT: MATTHEW 5:9 ESV

Blessed are the peacemakers, for they shall be called sons of God.

Rainbow Reflection: Share

Individuals with exceptionalities seem to be vigilant and aware of others.

One young man with ADHD is always prepared and comments, "I like it when we keep goodie bags and gloves in our car so I can pass them out to people who don't have food or a home."

SCRIPTURE SUPPORT: MATTHEW 25:35 ESV

For I was hungry, and you gave me food, I was thirsty, and you gave me drink, I was a stranger and you welcomed me.

Rainbow Reflection: Recognize Your Gifts and Use Them Wisely

We often undervalue, underestimate, and overlook our gifts. But even the smallest talent must be shared.

Drew and others demonstrate how simple gestures such as sharing a rainbow, or a smile can greatly impact others.

He and so many individuals with exceptionalities never complain about what they don't have, but rejoice, celebrate, and share what they do have.

The simplicity yet awareness of Drew's comment, "God made me special, because he showed me how to make rainbows," inspires me to be aware and to share.

SCRIPTURE SUPPORT: 2 PETER 1:10

Therefore, brothers, be all the more diligent to make your calling and election sure,
for if you practice these qualities you will never fall.

Rainbow Reflection:
Seek Forgiveness

Drew reminds me the importance of asking forgiveness. He says, "First I told Daddy I was sorry, and then I told God."

SCRIPTURE SUPPORT: 1 JOHN 1:9 ESV

If we confess our sins, he is faithful and just to forgive us our sins and to cleanse us from all unrighteousness.

Rainbow Reflection:
Remember to Offer It Up to God

The advice to "ask and ye shall receive," is not lost on Drew. He asks, "When I said my prayers, I asked God to help me."

SCRIPTURE SUPPORT: PHILIPPIANS 4:13 ESV

I can do all things through him who strengthens me.

Rainbow Reflection:
Take Care of One Another

A classmate with a hearing impairment comments, "They said he is sick; how can we help?" The empathy and desire to help is so apparent and inspirational.

SCRIPTURE SUPPORT: JAMES 5:14 ESV

Is anyone among you sick? Let him call for the elders of the church, and let them pray over him, anointing him with oil in the name of the Lord.

Rainbow Reflection: Forgive One Another

Drew never holds a grudge. The minute we apologize, Drew immediately says, "It's okay."

There is no drama, no silent treatment, no pouting, no cold shoulder; we simply hug and move on. It is something to behold.

SCRIPTURE SUPPORT: COLOSSIANS 3:13 ESV

Bearing with one another and, if one has a complaint against another, forgiving each other, as the Lord has forgiven you, so you also must forgive.

JUNE 20

Rainbow Reflection:
Share Time

Time with Dad is cherished by Drew. "My dad takes me to lots of sports and we sometimes get donuts; we have fun."

SCRIPTURE SUPPORT: ACTS 2:46 ESV

And day by day, attending the temple together and breaking bread in their homes they received their food with glad and generous hearts.

Rainbow Reflection: Include Humor in Your Daily Life

Drew is very literal, and his cousin Coleman and he have an ongoing joke about bath bombs. Of course, these are not real bombs, but shaped scents or bubbles that you add to a bath.

To Drew they just might be real, and he nervously says, "I like to take baths and Coleman jokes with me and says he's going to get me bath bombs, but that sounds scary because I don't want bombs in my bathtub."

Sometimes Cole will just call and say into the phone, "Bath bombs, bath bombs," to which Drew cracks up and runs around shouting, *"No, no, Coleman, I don't want those!"*

Their jokes and banter always create lighthearted laughter.

SCRIPTURE SUPPORT: ZEPHANIAH 3:17

The Lord your God is in your midst, a mighty one who will save; he will rejoice over you with gladness; he will quiet you by his love; he will exult over you with loud singing.

Rainbow Reflection: Share with Others

The simplicity of how many exceptional individuals view the world makes life less complicated. Drew states, "I share my toy football helmets because God wants us to share; it is just that easy."

SCRIPTURE SUPPORT: LUKE 3:11 ESV

And he answered them, "Whoever has two tunics is to share with him who has none, and whoever has food is to do likewise."

JUNE 23

Rainbow Reflection:
See Your Beauty

I complain to Drew as another birthday approaches, "Growing older is no fun."

Drew replies, "No, Mommy, don't say that; you are not old, you are beautiful!"

I reply, "No, Drew, you are beautiful, and thank you for always seeing the best in me."

SCRIPTURE SUPPORT: 2 CORINTHIANS 4:16-17 ESV

So we do not lose heart. Though our outer self is wasting away, our inner self is being renewed day by day.

Rainbow Reflection:
Remember That work and a Profession
Are So Much More Than a Paycheck

Drew was hired to work for a wonderful community that serves the elderly. He works three two-hour shifts a week and he is very proud of this accomplishment. He recently came home from work beaming and waving an envelope.

"Are you ready for it, Mom? You are going to love this. My boss said I am doing a great job!"

I admire and wish for more companies to hire individuals with exceptionalities who bring so much to the workforce.

Hiring an individual with exceptionalities is mutually beneficial. While Drew gains income and a sense of accomplishment, he also brings a different perspective that motivates other employees and even residents of the retirement community.

Learning from one another is an integral part to the fabric of society and that is what a diverse and inclusive workplace supports.

Drew says, "I am so proud of my job, and with my paycheck maybe I'll treat the family to some Graeter's ice cream."

Exceptional.

JUNE 25

Rainbow Reflection:
Make Time to Be Together

Drew is the happiest when his family is together. When one of the family members is away, it makes Drew somewhat anxious and he counts down until we are all together again.

"Only 17 days until Sissy is home from college, Mommy. Only 16 days until Sissy comes home from college, Mommy. Only 15 days…"

SCRIPTURE SUPPORT: PSALMS 133:1 ESV

A song of Ascents. Of David. Behold, how good and pleasant
it is when brothers dwell in unity!

Rainbow Reflection:
Stick Up for Others

Elaina greatly values her friends and their loyalty. She states, "If my little people friends see someone talking behind my back, they stick up for me and that makes me feel so good."

SCRIPTURE SUPPORT: 1 THESSALONIANS 5:15 ESV

See that no one repays anyone evil for evil, but always seek to do good to one another and to everyone.

Rainbow Reflection:
Believe in Yourself

John has Williams syndrome, but that did not stop him! He manifested winning the top award in his high school, which no individual with exceptionalities had ever earned.

His belief in himself was apparent and contagious. He shares, "I made history for the special education program when I was selected out of the entire senior class for the Cavalier Award. This is the highest honor at our school and recognizes an outstanding student who exemplifies excellence and makes a difference in the community. I was the first special education student to ever receive this award. You see, you can achieve anything you put your mind to!"

SCRIPTURE SUPPORT: 2 TIMOTHY 4:7 ESV

I have fought the good fight, I have finished the race, I have kept the faith.

JUNE 28

Rainbow Reflection:
Create Coping Mechanisms

Drew must dig deep for courage and strength whenever both parents travel. It is uncommon, but when it occurs, Drew soothes himself by saying, "It will be alright. Mommy and Daddy will be back in a few days and that is not long; it will be okay, and Grandma and I can play cards."

I see him growing up and managing events that challenge his comfort zone. This is lifelong skill that will serve him well.

SCRIPTURE SUPPORT: MATTHEW 6:34

Therefore, do not be anxious about tomorrow, for tomorrow will be anxious for itself. Sufficient for the day is its own trouble.

Rainbow Reflection:
Enjoy the Arts

Dakota is an amazing artist and draws beautiful pictures that often reflect her feelings. She also finds comfort and healing in other art forms and comments, "Music makes my heart happy."

SCRIPTURE SUPPORT: JOB 21:12 ESV

They sing to the tambourine and the lyre and rejoice to the sound of the pipe.

Rainbow Reflection: Cherish All Friendships

I've noticed that most individuals with exceptionalities don't notice appearance, race, status, creed, intellect, etc.

Whether interacting with humans or animals, they seem to be above the fray and see beyond the obvious.

Drew shares, "When I look into my dog Maggie's eyes, I see she loves me, and I love her; Maggie is a good friend."

SCRIPTURE SUPPORT: MATTHEW 6:26 ESV

Look at the birds of the air; they neither sow nor reap nor gather into barns, and yet your heavenly Father feeds them; are you not of more value than they?

Rainbow Reflection: Find Renewal in Each New Day and Give Thanks

Drew reminds me to take a minute and stop rushing. When he encourages me to slow down to take in the day, it provides a calm and pause, and I'm so grateful.

"Mommy, isn't it a beautiful morning?"

SCRIPTURE SUPPORT: JOB 38:7 ESV

When the morning stars sang together, and all the sons of God shouted for joy.

Rainbow Reflection: Share Your Talents

Drew shares a new love for painting and comments, "My dad teaches me how to paint. I made a special painting for my friend who was sick with cancer. She said she looked at it a lot and it helped her feel better."

SCRIPTURE SUPPORT: LUKE 6:38 ESV

Give, and it will be given to you. Good measure, pressed down, shaken together, running over, will be put into your lap. For with the measure you use it will be measured back to you.

Rainbow Reflection: Share in Other Passions

Andrew delights in live theater and this is especially true when his sister Alexandra is on the stage. His excitement always encourages her. "Alexandra, only twelve more days until your show; I can't wait to see you!"

SCRIPTURE SUPPORT: PHILIPPIANS 2:3-4 ESV

Do nothing from rivalry or conceit, but in humility count others more significant than yourselves. Let each of you look not only to his own interests, but also to the interests of others.

Rainbow Reflection:
Thank Service Men and Women

Without prompting, when Drew sees service men and women in the community he commonly says, "Thank you for your service, and I think you are very brave."

SCRIPTURE SUPPORT: RUTH 2:12 ESV

"The Lord repay you for what you have done, and a full reward be given you by the Lord, the God of Israel, under whose wings you have come to take refuge!"

Rainbow Reflection:
Serve Others

Drew inherently recognizes the needs of others. As his grandmother is aging and memory sometimes eludes her, he always cares for her. In fact, I often refer to them as "peas and carrots" because he cares for her, and she cares for him.

Drew says, "I like to do nice things for Grandma, because it is sweet to do so."

SCRIPTURE SUPPORT: COLOSSIANS 3:12 ESV

Put on then, as God's chosen ones, holy and beloved, compassionate hearts, kindness, humility, meekness and patience.

Rainbow Reflection: Take Care of Yourself

Often individuals with exceptionalities are very in touch with their needs.

One friend with ADHD comments, "I have to get some rest, or I might get crabby."

SCRIPTURE SUPPORT: PROVERBS 3:24

If you lie down, you will not be afraid; when you lie down, your sleep will be sweet.

Rainbow Reflection:
Take Time to Be Together

Drew recognizes and reminds me the importance of community as he comments, "When my whole family is together, I feel comfortable, but when we are away from one another, it is hard, and I feel kind of sad."

SCRIPTURE SUPPORT: PHILIPPIANS 2:2

Complete my joy by being of the same mind, having the same love, being in full accord and of one mind.

Rainbow Reflection: Keep Order in Your Life

Routine and order seem very important to many individuals with exceptionalities despite the diagnosis.

Drew is VERY routine. He shares, "When my markers are out of order, it makes me uncomfortable, so I have to fix them; I like things to be in order."

SCRIPTURE SUPPORT: 1 CORINTHIANS 14:40 ESV

But all things should be done decently and in order.

JULY 9

Rainbow Reflection:
Be Loving

Drew and so many exceptional people demonstrate joy and exude love and it comes so naturally to them. Drew continually ponders, "I just wish everyone would love one another like God says we should."

SCRIPTURE SUPPORT: 1 JOHN 4:11 ESV

Beloved, if God so loved us, we also ought to love one another.

Rainbow Reflection:
Be Dedicated

Drew recognizes that his father is loving and dedicated. He shares, "I love Daddy. In the morning, he helps me get ready because he gels my hair and helps me shave; he is a good Daddy."

SCRIPTURE SUPPORT: ROMANS 12:13

Contribute to the needs of the saints and seek to show hospitality.

Rainbow Reflection:
Seek Peace

A friend with Down syndrome provides great advice: "People should not have violence and they should be more loving; that is what Jesus says."

SCRIPTURE SUPPORT: MATTHEW 26: 52-54

Then Jesus said to him, "Put your sword back into its place. For all who take the sword will perish by the sword. Do you think that I cannot appeal to my father, and he will at once send me more than twelve legions of angels? But how then should the Scriptures be fulfilled, that I must be so?"

Rainbow Reflection:
Share Your Gifts

Drew feels that everyone is special because everyone has gifts and something unique to offer. His perspective has taught me that no matter how big or small our gifts or talents may seem, it is important to share them with others.

"Jesus told me that he was proud of me that I made my rainbows and that I shared them with everyone."

SCRIPTURE SUPPORT: 1 TIMOTHY 4:14 ESV

Do not neglect the gift you have, which was given you by prophecy when the council of elders laid their hands on you.

Rainbow Reflection:
Listen for God's Voice

I have realized that life can get so busy and hectic that I don't have capacity to hear Jesus calling. Drew always seems to be listening: "Jesus called my name, so I ran over."

SCRIPTURE SUPPORT: PROVERBS 2:2

Making your ear attentive to wisdom and inclining your heart to understanding.

Rainbow Reflection:
Dote on One Another

Drew cherishes his Aunt JuJu, who has been a constant source of love and spoiling in his life.

As time passes, Drew's appreciation for JuJu deepens and he tries to spoil her with notes, signs, and phone calls.

"I miss JuJu because I love her, and she spoils me, and she always gets me cheese coneys. We should spoil Aunt Juju."

SCRIPTURE SUPPORT: 2 CORINTHIANS 9:7 ESV

Each one must give as he has decided in his heart, not reluctantly or under compulsion, for God loves a cheerful giver.

Rainbow Reflection:
Always Be Respectful

A player on the Special Olympics basketball team reminds his teammates, "When the game is over, we should congratulate each other because someone has to win, and someone has to lose."

SCRIPTURE SUPPORT: LUKE 6:35

But love your enemies, and do good, and lend, expecting nothing in return, and your reward will be great, and you will be sons of the Most High, for he is kind to the ungrateful and the evil.

Rainbow Reflection:
Keep Traditions Alive

Traditions are important, especially for exceptional individuals who value routine. Drew says, "I can't wait to go on vacation with all of the cousins. I like that we go every other year, because it is fun to spend time and play on the beach."

SCRIPTURE SUPPORT: 2 THESSALONIANS 2:15 ESV

So then, brothers, stand firm and hold to the traditions that you were taught by us, either by our spoken word or by tour letter.

Rainbow Reflection:
Share Good News

"**I** loved putting my rainbows all over our house for everyone to see," Drew proudly comments.

SCRIPTURE SUPPORT: MATTHEW 5:16 ESV

"In the same way, let your light shine before others, so that they may see your good works and give glory to your Father who is in heaven."

Rainbow Reflection: Love Yourself

John, who has Williams syndrome, is so wise. He shares, "If one is not happy with themselves, one is thinking the wrong way. You need to feel rich inside and love yourself."

SCRIPTURE SUPPORT: 2 CORINTHIANS 13:14

The grace of the Lord Jesus Christ and the love of God and the fellowship of the Holy Spirit be with you all.

Rainbow Reflection:
Trust and Rest in the Palm of His Hand

I've heard faith that is awe inspiring from children with exception-alities. "I don't worry because God will take care of it for me," Drew confidently states.

SCRIPTURE SUPPORT: 1 PETER 5:7 ESV

Casting all your anxieties on him, because he cares for you.

Rainbow Reflection:
Share a Compliment Today

"It is a good idea to give compliments," states a friend who suffers with seizures.

SCRIPTURE SUPPORT: PROVERBS 27:2 ESV

Let another praise you, and not your own mouth, a stranger, and not your own lips.

JULY 21

Rainbow Reflection: Be a Refuge for Someone

"If I'm out in public and people make fun of me for being different, I don't look at them, and I hide behind my mom and dad; I feel safe under their protection." An important reminder from a friend with exceptionalities to take care of one another.

SCRIPTURE SUPPORT: EPHESIANS 6:11 ESV

Put on the whole armor of God, that you may be able
to stand against the schemes of the devil.

Rainbow Reflection: Pray for One Another

"I said a prayer for you, Mommy," Drew comments. He always prays for others before himself.

SCRIPTURE SUPPORT: JAMES 5:16 ESV

Therefore, confess your sins to one another and pray for one another, that you may be healed. The prayer of a righteous person has great power as it is working.

Rainbow Reflection:
Deny Evil

"The devil is a bad guy and God is all LOVE." Drew's simple statement easily delineates good and evil.

SCRIPTURE SUPPORT: JAMES 4:7 ESV

Submit yourselves therefore to God. Resist the devil, and he will flee from you.

Rainbow Reflection:
Take Private Time for Yourself

Our cousin with exceptionalities recognizes when a personal "time out" is necessary. He says, "When I feel sad, I go to my room and read Sports Illustrated. It feels good to read that and have alone time."

SCRIPTURE SUPPORT: PSALMS 46:10 ESV

"Be still and know that I am God. I will be exalted among the nations; I will be exalted in the earth!"

Rainbow Reflection:
Find Comfort

Drew admits, "Now that I'm big, some people say I should get rid of Teddy, but I will never give him up; I can't help it, because I love Teddy so much!"

SCRIPTURE SUPPORT: PSALMS 119-9 ESV

How can a young man keep his way pure? By guarding it according to your word.

Rainbow Reflection: Calm Yourself

Drew has learned the importance of coping skills. Now he is quick to share his tips and ideas with others, "When I know a friend or family member is sad or upset, I help them to count to twenty to calm down or make them laugh."

SCRIPTURE SUPPORT: PROVERBS 24:10 ESV

If you faint in the day of adversity, your strength is small.

Rainbow Reflection: Participate

A good reminder not to let life pass you by. Drew comments, "I like to dance, and I love to sing in church, and it is fun to sing with others. You should always try to participate."

SCRIPTURE SUPPORT: PSALMS 147:1 ESV

Praise the LORD! For it is good to sing praises to our God;
for it is pleasant, and a song of praise is fitting.

Rainbow Reflection: Move Beyond Your Comfort Zone

A reminder from a friend who has more challenges than most but continues to push himself beyond his comfort zone. He shares, "Sometimes you might be scared, but you just have to go for things."

SCRIPTURE SUPPORT: PSALMS 34:4

I sought the Lord, and he answered me and delivered me from all my fears.

Rainbow Reflection: Cherish People

The red-carpet premiere of the short documentary Drew Gets It will be a highlight of our life.

The community support was overwhelming as friends, family and strangers came to the sold-out event of over 500 attendees.

The impact was not lost on Drew, who commented, "It felt good to have so many people come to see the documentary and I had so much fun!"

Cincinnati is a very special town with exceptional people on all levels.

SCRIPTURE SUPPORT: HEBREWS 13:1 ESV

Let brotherly love continue.

Rainbow Reflection: Give Praise

Drew loves Jesus and often says, "If I could talk to Jesus, I would tell him he was the best person that ever was on this world."

SCRIPTURE SUPPORT: JOHN 14:6 ESV

Jesus said to him, "I am the way, and the truth, and the life. No one comes to the Father except through me."

Rainbow Reflection:
Find Peace in Nature

Drew talks of his love for his grandma and nature when he says, "Grandma Leurck loves nature and likes to take us camping; I love going camping, I love having campfires, and I love Grandma!"

SCRIPTURE SUPPORT: LUKE 6:12 ESV

In these days he went out to the mountain to pray,
and all night he continued in prayer to God.

AUGUST 1

Rainbow Reflection: Don't Give Up

"Sometimes it is hard, but you just have to keep trying." A good reminder from a friend with cerebal palsy.

SCRIPTURE SUPPORT: ROMANS 5:3 ESV

More than that, we rejoice in our sufferings, knowing that suffering produces endurance.

Rainbow Reflection:
Stay Calm

"When I get mad, Mommy says to take three deep breaths. When I do, I feel better and more at peace." Drew has learned that calm prevails.

SCRIPTURE SUPPORT: PROVERBS 29:11

A fool gives full vent to his spirit, but a wise man quietly holds it back.

Rainbow Reflection: Try Something New

As Drew gets older and taller, expectations grow, and because there is no physical sign of the cognitive delay, there is often a disconnect for people who interact with Drew.

At age fifteen, Drew is turning into a handsome young man. He is tall, with blue eyes and a big smile that lights up his face; he is also noticing girls.

On a beach trip, Drew plays with his Star Wars figurines in the sand as I sit reading a few feet away. I notice Drew's head almost fall off his shoulders as he notices two beautiful girls, about his age, walking in his direction.

He quickly stands up to greet them and say hello.

The girls flirtatiously respond, "Hey there, how are you doing?"

I can tell they think he is cute, and they are happy to chat with him.

Drew immediately responds, "Do you want to play Star Wars, guys?" The girls are a bit perplexed at his invitation. Impressively, Drew reads their body language and quickly pivots, "Or if you don't like Star Wars, we can play Power Rangers."

The beautiful girls seem to connect the dots and politely respond, "You are so sweet, but we are going to go on ahead walking. But we will be sure to say hello on our way back."

They were kind, but my heart sank as I realized we were entering another stage. Drew, on the other hand went back to happily playing and said, "Did you see that, Mommy? I made two new friends."

SCRIPTURE SUPPORT: 1 CORINTHIANS 16:7

For I do not want to see you now just in passing.
I hope to spend some time with you, if the Lord permits.

Rainbow Reflection:
Choose the Side of Good

Drew reminds me of life's most important lessons. "Why can't everyone just be good, have fun with each other, and do the right thing? That would make God so happy."

SCRIPTURE SUPPORT: MATTHEW 5:8 ESV

"Blessed are the pure in heart, for they shall see God.

Rainbow Reflection:

A good friend of Drew's with Asperger's contemplates, "Maybe give back a little bit to find true happiness."

SCRIPTURE SUPPORT: PROVERBS 19:17 ESV

Whoever is generous to the poor lends to the Lord,
and he will repay him for his deed.

AUGUST 6

Rainbow Reflection: Recognize God in Nature

Nature is calming to so many, but individuals with exceptionalities often seek its respite and a change in demeanor and mood often follow.

Drew comments, "When I am at the lake or with nature, I feel at peace, like nothing can hurt me."

SCRIPTURE SUPPORT: PSALMS 145:5 ESV

On the glorious splendor of your majesty, and on your wondrous works,
I will meditate.

Rainbow Reflection: Utilize Coping Skills

At a graduation party for a classmate with exceptionalities, the graduate admitted, "School was hard and at times I felt over-whelmed, so I took breaks, and counted to ten, but I am proud that I graduated."

SCRIPTURE SUPPORT: JOB 33:4 ESV

The Spirit of God has made me, and the breath of the Almighty gives me life.

Rainbow Reflection:
Respect One Another

Drew is surrounded by men of excellence who have modeled chivalry, and Drew has been a good student. "If I go on a date with a girl, I will treat her real nice; I will open the door and give her my arm to hold onto when I go on a date."

SCRIPTURE SUPPORT: ROMANS 12:10 ESV

Love one another with brotherly affection. Outdo one another showing honor.

AUGUST 9

Rainbow Reflection:
Give Someone a Chance

Drew was never the star player when he played Cougar Football, but he became a star teammate to many players and several of his coaches. The letter below was sent from his coach to our family at Christmas and is a priceless gift I continue to cherish.

I just want to let you know that coaching Andrew was a special experience that I never expected. I got so much more out of it than I ever returned to him. Football is the hardest sport to play and coach. I believe that I have an obligation to prepare the kids to minimize their chances of hurting themselves or their teammates. I don't believe in cutting anyone slack. From the beginning I was very concerned with Andrew. I could see that there was no way I could protect him, and I was worried that he was going to be a distraction.

As the season went on, I began to notice how special he was to the team. I saw how his teammates really cared about him. They went out of their way in the drills to make sure that he did not get hurt. Regardless of the score, they were truly excited for him when he got in games. They took it upon themselves to make sure that he was in the right place, knew what to do, and was going to be safe. They cheered his every play. They were very concerned when he got hurt. He gave this team a heart, a spirit.

I also began to notice how important it was for him to be a member of the team and how proud he was to put on his Cougar uniform. He never knew what it was like to throw a great block, score a touchdown, or make a game-saving tackle. But, just like the kids who played every play, he glowed in the victories and hurt in the losses. These are things the rest of us take for granted.

I also enjoyed our impromptu conversations, whether it was on the side-lines or between drills at practice. He always made me laugh. He really is a special kid and I treasure the experience I had coaching him. Who said you can't teach an old dog new tricks? Please tell him I said Hi.

Hope you and your family have a great holiday season.

Thanks,
Coach

SCRIPTURE SUPPORT: PHILIPPIANS 2:3 ESV

Do nothing from rivalry or conceit, but in humility count others more significant than yourselves.

AUGUST 10

Rainbow Reflection: Respect Your Mind, Body, and Spirit

A dear friend with Asperger syndrome understands what helps him feel his best. He shares, "Exercise and sports calm me down."

SCRIPTURE SUPPORT: 1 CORINTHIANS 6:19-20 ESV

Or do you not know that your body is a temple of the Holy Spirit within you, whom you have from God? You are not your own, for you were bought with a price. So, glorify God in your body.

AUGUST 11

Rainbow Reflection:
Affirm Others

In high school, Drew was in a program that focused on life skills and employment. He practiced building a resume, interviewing, and on the job duties. He was accepted at Walgreens and we were so proud of him.

Being a parent of a child with exceptionalities is full of surprises and sometimes I disappoint myself.

I went to visit Drew at work and without him realizing I was there, I watched from afar as he stocked shelves and checked expiration dates.

After several minutes, I had to run out to the car and quickly shut the door. I put my head on the steering wheel and quietly sobbed. Seeing my firstborn working so diligently stocking shelves, I had mixed emotions.

I was so grateful that he was given this opportunity, but the ugly monster of comparison creeped into my small mind of other school friends who were graduating and heading to college, playing sports, and getting scholarships while Drew was stocking shelves.

I gave myself about ten minutes, then took a deep breath and flipped the switch from comparison to gratitude and thanked God for Drew's health, his physicality, and his abilities, not his challenges. I asked for forgiveness for once again being so weak. Not a proud moment, but a real moment.

I went back in and met Drew with a big smile and told him the truth about just how proud I was of him. I met his manager who said Drew was such a pleasure to have in the store and that he was doing such a great job.

That evening at dinner I told the family how well Drew was doing at work and Drew said, "When they told me at Walgreens that they wanted to hire me, I felt so proud and happy."

I am a work in progress, and I continue to strive to do better.

SCRIPTURE SUPPORT: 1 THESSALONIANS 5:11-14

Therefore encourage one another and build one another up, just as you are doing. We ask you, brothers, to respect those who labor among you and are over you in the Lord and admonish you, and to esteem them very highly in love because of their work. Be at peace among yourselves. And we urge you, brothers, admonish the idle, encourage the fainthearted, help the weak, be patient with them all.

Rainbow Reflection: Love and Learn from Everyone in the Community

Drew cherishes his parents and grandparents and listens closely to those older than him. He is considerate, interested, and always takes time to interact with people of all ages.

"God says you should love your mother and father, and that is easy; besides, I already knew that one!"

SCRIPTURE SUPPORT: PROVERBS 1:8-9 ESV

Hear, my son, your father's instruction, and forsake not your mother's teaching, for they are a graceful garland for your head and pendants for your neck.

Rainbow Reflection:
Recognize the Power of Kindness

My experience with exceptional children is that they have kind and thoughtful hearts.

Drew said, "Today I surprised Mommy and I brought her coffee in bed, and for some reason she smiled and cried. It felt good to be kind."

SCRIPTURE SUPPORT: GALATIANS 5:22 ESV

But the fruit of the Spirit is love, joy, peace, patience, kindness, goodness, faithfulness.

Rainbow Reflection: Encourage Others

Drew enjoys playing sports, but he gets as much enjoyment out of seeing friends and family in the stands. "When I look in the crowd and see my family holding the sign to cheer me on, it makes my heart so happy."

SCRIPTURE SUPPORT: ROMANS 12:15 ESV

Rejoice with those who rejoice, weep with those who weep.

AUGUST 15

Rainbow Reflection: Distract Yourself from Worry

Many exceptional children have mastered coping skills and create proactive solutions to manage stress. A friend with Autism comments, "Sometimes I play my video games and I forget to worry."

SCRIPTURE SUPPORT: MATTHEW 6:34 ESV

"Therefore, do not be anxious about tomorrow, for tomorrow will be anxious for itself. Sufficient for the day is its own trouble."

Rainbow Reflection: Trust in God's Plan for You

Most people daydream about the future, but individuals with exceptionalities often inspire me to dream bigger. "If I could talk to Jesus, I would ask him, what will I be when I grow up? He would probably say a Reds player, a Bengals quarterback, or a zookeeper."

SCRIPTURE SUPPORT: JEREMIAH 29:11 ESV

For I know the plans I have for you, declares the Lord, plans for welfare and not for evil, to give you a future and a hope.

Rainbow Reflection: Check In on Friends

Empathy seems to come natural to individuals with exceptionalities. A relative with dwarfism comments, "When I see a friend is sad, I ask if they are okay."

SCRIPTURE SUPPORT: 1 PETER 3:8

Finally, all of you, have unity of mind, sympathy, brotherly love,
a tender heart and a humble mind.

AUGUST 18

Rainbow Reflection: Teach Others

Regardless of capabilities, it is important to teach as well as to learn. Drew says, "Mommy shaves me, but she says that it is time that I learn to do it for myself. I'm learning new things just like I teach my little sister new things."

SCRIPTURE SUPPORT: PROVERBS 16:16 ESV

How much better to get wisdom than gold!
To get understanding is to be chosen rather than silver.

Rainbow Reflection: Overdeliver

Since the age of seven, Drew has made me a rainbow every day. Rarely does a day go by that I don't receive his beautiful drawing.

"It is only February 1st but guess what, I made you rainbows for all of the days in February," Drew excitedly exclaims.

"Drew, don't you ever get tired of making me rainbows?" I reply.

With the sweetest smile Drew responds, "No, Mommy, because you love them."

SCRIPTURE SUPPORT: PROVERBS 11:25 ESV

Whoever brings blessing will be enriched,
and one who waters will himself be watered.

Rainbow Reflection:
Reassure One Another Even If You Don't
Have All of the Answers

"Sometimes I don't know what to say, so I just say, it will be okay," shares a friend with ADHD.

SCRIPTURE SUPPORT: PSALMS 34:7

The angel of the Lord encamps around those who fear him and delivers them.

Rainbow Reflection:
Share Your Blessings with Others

NiNi is a best friend who is like an aunt to Drew. He loves her and he loves visiting her lake house.

"Mommy, NiNi is like family because she lets me come to her lake house, she takes me tubing, and she loves me. She is always giving me good food, and I love her sandwich bar!"

SCRIPTURE SUPPORT: GALATIANS 6:6 ESV

One who is taught the word must share all good things with the one who teaches.

AUGUST 22

Rainbow Reflection: Have Faith in Yourself

Some of the most determined and self-assured humans I meet are individuals with exceptionalities. So often doubting oneself is an easy trap to fall into, but this rarely happens for Drew. He believes anything is possible. "With your love and God's love, I believe I can do anything!"

SCRIPTURE SUPPORT: ISAIAH 41:10

Fear not, for I am with you; be not dismayed, for I am your God; I will strengthen you, I will help you, I will uphold you with my righteous right hand.

AUGUST 23

Rainbow Reflection: Recognize the Human Experience Is Shared, and the Common Denominator Is Love

Exceptional individuals want others to see them and not their disability. A friend with Williams syndrome says, "It makes me sad when people look at me differently; I am just like everyone else."

SCRIPTURE SUPPORT: 1 JOHN 4:20 ESV

If anyone says, "I love God," and hates his brother, he is a liar; for he who does not love his brother whom he has seen cannot love God whom he has not seen.

Rainbow Reflection:
Reach Out to One Another with Love

On a recent trip to the Outer Banks, we were out to dinner and I noticed Drew talking with the waiter at the end of the table. They seemed to be having a nice conversation and I noticed Drew gave him a rainbow card. As we were settling our bill, the waiter came up and commented how much he enjoyed talking with Drew. We chatted a few minutes, thanked him, and went on our way.

A week later, we got an unexpected email from our waiter:

"I believe Drew was sent to me that night to remind me of what's most important...life. Not just existing but living. I'm an emotional person and yes, Drew made me cry.

"I still have the card he gave me, and I'll hold onto it forever. Its meaning is richer than any size dollar bill to me."

SCRIPTURE SUPPORT: PSALMS 23: 1-6

A Psalm of David. The Lord is my shepherd; I shall not want. He makes me lie down in green pastures. He leads me beside still waters. He restores my soul. He leads me in paths of righteousness for his name›s sake. Even though I walk through the valley of the shadow of death, I will fear no evil, for you are with me; your rod and your staff, they comfort me. You prepare a table before me in the presence of my enemies; you anoint my head with oil; my cup overflows. ...

Rainbow Reflection:
Seek Comfort Through Shared Experiences

A child with dwarfism comments, "My little people friends make me happy because we go through similar things; they get it, and that makes me feel so happy."

SCRIPTURE SUPPORT: EPHESIANS 4:32

Be kind to one another, tenderhearted,
forgiving one another as God in Christ forgave you.

Rainbow Reflection:
Seek Support When Needed

"If I'm at school and people are picking on me, I tell a teacher."

SCRIPTURE SUPPORT: PROVERBS 11:14 ESV

Where there is no guidance, a people fall,
but in an abundance of counselors there is safety.

Rainbow Reflection:
Remember Loved Ones

I sit in awe at how Drew processes death. He acknowledges missing a loved one, but he places greater emphasis on his unwavering trust that the loved one is rejoicing in heaven.

"I miss Uncle David, but I know he is in heaven."

SCRIPTURE SUPPORT: JOHN 5:24 ESV

Truly, truly, I say to you, whoever hears my word and believes
him who send me has eternal life. He does not come into judgement
but has passed from death to life.

Rainbow Reflection:
See Everyone's Gifts

"**M**ommy, people say I am special, but I think that everyone is special."

Today, August 28, is Drew's birthday; thank you Jesus for the gift of our son.

SCRIPTURE SUPPORT: PSALMS 139:14 ESV

I praise you, for I am fearfully and wonderfully made. Wonderful are your works;
my soul knows it very well.

Rainbow Reflection:
Be Tenderhearted and Caring to Others

Drew is a romantic. He often talks about girls, and he takes pride in chivalrous behavior.

I often overhear him daydream, "I'm not sure who I will marry, but I might like to get married one day. I would hold the door open for my bride and take very good care of her."

SCRIPTURE SUPPORT: HEBREWS 10:24 ESV

And let us consider how to stir up one another to love and good works.

Rainbow Reflection:
Be the Light in Someone's Day

"When I see a friend that is feeling down, I come over and ask what is wrong. Then I try to make them smile and tell a joke."

SCRIPTURE SUPPORT: LUKE 6:31 ESV

And as you wish that others would do to you, do so to them

Rainbow Reflection:
See the Beauty in the Weeds

Every spring and still to this day, Drew picks every dandelion he sees as we walk in the neighborhood. Most people consider dandelions to be weeds and do everything to rid them from their yards. Drew sees them differently.

"Close your eyes, Mommy, I have a surprise for you; it is your beautiful flower," and then he hands me a dandelion weed.

SCRIPTURE SUPPORT: 1 JOHN 3:18 ESV

Little children, let us not love in word or talk but indeed and in truth.

Rainbow Reflection:
Be Someone's Biggest Fan

Drew loves watching his sister Audrey play sports. "Audrey, you are my superstar and I am your biggest fan. You are the best rower a brother could ever ask for!"

SCRIPTURE SUPPORT: HEBREWS 10:24 ESV

And let us consider how to stir up one another to love and good works.

Rainbow Reflection:
Try New Things

"I am proud I try new things. I was afraid of the big camel Hercules but by the end of our ride, we were friends."

SCRIPTURE SUPPORT: EZRA 10:4 ESV

Arise, for it is your task, and we are with you; be strong and do it.

SEPTEMBER 3

Rainbow Reflection: Put In the Effort

On days I feel overwhelmed or not up for the challenge, I can always count on Drew to reassure me, "Mommy, just go out and be glorious today!"

SCRIPTURE SUPPORT: DANIEL 12:3 ESV

And those who are wise shall shine like the brightness of the sky above; and those who turn many to righteousness, like the stars forever and ever.

Rainbow Reflection: Be Dedicated

"Uncle Steve works hard for his family, he even had to leave on Christmas to do his job." Drew is always paying attention. He appreciates and notices the little things, especially dedication.

SCRIPTURE SUPPORT: COLOSSIANS 3:23-24 ESV

Whatever you do, work heartily, as for the Lord and not for men,
knowing that from the Lord you will receive the inheritance as your reward.
You are serving the Lord Christ.

Rainbow Reflection:
Be Collaborative

Andrew reminds me of the importance of collaboration and pride in work.

"It makes me smile to work with friends at my job; we work together, and we make a good team. Sometimes they try to help me but I tell them I can do it, because I also want to show them how I can do it all by myself."

SCRIPTURE SUPPORT: ECCLESIASTES 4:9-12 ESV

Two are better than one, because they have a good reward for their toil. For if they fall, one will lift up his fellow. But woe to him who is alone when he falls and has not another to lift him up!

Rainbow Reflection:
Expect Positive Outcomes

My father was a great man. He was an eternal optimist and from the moment the challenges and diagnosis began to pour in about Drew, his opinion did not waver: his grandson was perfect.

At some of my lowest moments, my father's reassurance gave me the strength to parent Drew through love, hope, and acceptance. I miss my father terribly, but I am forever grateful for his belief in Drew.

Drew was also aware of his grandfather's opinion, and it provided a sense of pride and confidence to him.

I often tear up when Drew comments, "Grandfather says I am perfect, nothing is wrong with me, and I will be just fine. I smile when I think of Grandfather."

SCRIPTURE SUPPORT: PSALMS 37:5 ESV

Commit your way to the Lord; trust in him, and he will act.

Rainbow Reflection: Have Fun

Having fun and experiencing joy come naturally to most exceptional individuals, and they seem to have less inhibitions.

A friend with ADHD and a cognition delay is always up for fun. She says, "Karaoke makes me happy because everyone gets together, and we sing."

SCRIPTURE SUPPORT: PSALMS 95: 1-2

Oh come, let us sing to the Lord; let us make a joyful noise to the rock of our salvation! Let us come into his presence with thanksgiving; let us make a joyful noise to him with songs of praise!

Rainbow Reflection:
Be a Haven to Others

"Loved ones make me feel safe; when I am afraid, I just have my family hold me and I feel so much better."

SCRIPTURE SUPPORT: ISAIAH 66:13 ESV

As one whom his mother comforts. So, I will comfort you;
you shall be comforted in Jerusalem.

Rainbow Reflection:
Love Yourself

"I'm happy to be me," said a friend with Down syndrome.

I'm inspired and wonder how many people could exclaim this statement?

SCRIPTURE SUPPORT: EPHESIANS 2:10

For we are his workmanship, created in Christ Jesus for good works, which God prepared beforehand, that we should walk in them.

Rainbow Reflection:
Give Back

There is very rarely any hesitation for Drew when it comes to the needs of others. If he sees a need he simply and quickly says, "We have to help."

SCRIPTURE SUPPORT: DEUTERONOMY 22:4 ESV

You shall not see your brother's donkey, or his ox fallen down by the way and ignore them. You shall help him to lift them up again.

Rainbow Reflection: Show Honor

"When I visited NYC, I saw what happened on September 11th, and then I felt sad, and then I prayed; sometimes that is the best you can do," said Drew.

SCRIPTURE SUPPORT: PSALMS 34:18

The Lord is near to the brokenhearted and saves the crushed in spirit.

Rainbow Reflection: Make Time for Fun

"Just because I'm a little person, I'm still like everyone else. When I'm with my friends we do makeovers, make slime, and have fun; you know, girl stuff," said a relative with dwarfism.

SCRIPTURE SUPPORT: JOB 29:4 ESV

As I was in my prime, when the friendship of God was upon my tent.

SEPTEMBER 13

Rainbow Reflection:
Acknowledge Others' Gifts and Talents

"I feel good when people compliment my drawings," states Dakota when asked what she likes about being an artist.

SCRIPTURE SUPPORT: EPHESIANS 5:19 ESV

Addressing one another in Psalms and hymns and spiritual songs, singing and making melody.

Rainbow Reflection:
Get Out into Nature

Nature has a way to center the soul and a friend on the autism spectrum reminds me to get outside.

He shares, "At the lake I feel happy, calm, and relaxed."

SCRIPTURE SUPPORT: GENESIS 1:10 ESV

God called the dry land Earth, and the waters that were gathered together he called Seas. And God saw that it was good.

Rainbow Reflection: Remember That Actions Sometimes Speak Louder Than Words

"When a friend is sad, sometimes you don't have to say anything, and you just give them a hug," Drew reminds me.

SCRIPTURE SUPPORT: 1 JOHN 4:7-8 ESV

Beloved, let us love one another, for love is from God, and whoever loves has been born of God and knows God. Anyone who does not love does not know God, because God is love.

Rainbow Reflection: Look After One Another

Drew comments, "When my parents get tired of helping me or they die, my sisters are going to help me, and I'm so grateful for that."

SCRIPTURE SUPPORT: 1 CORINTHIANS 1:10 ESV

I appeal to you, brothers, by the name of our Lord Jesus Christ, that all of you agree, and that there be no divisions among you, but that you be united in the same mind and the same judgement.

Rainbow Reflection:
Love Animals

Drew says, "I'm so happy God gave me my new puppy."

He reminds me that animals are a gift that add companionship, comfort, and unconditional love; they are almost therapeutic.

SCRIPTURE SUPPORT: PSALMS 23:6 ESV

Surely goodness and mercy shall follow me all the days of my life, and I shall dwell in the house of the Lord forever.

Rainbow Reflection:
Comfort One Another

"When I see a friend that is sad, I tell them it is going to be okay and try to help them stay calm," says a friend with Down syndrome.

SCRIPTURE SUPPORT: 1 JOHN 4:18 ESV

There is no fear in love, but perfect love casts out fear. For fear has to do with punishment, and whoever fears has not been perfected in love.

Rainbow Reflection:
Embrace Change

Debbie is exceptional and she embraces change.

She says, "I like it every year when I see the relatives at Christmas parties. You know what happens is the little kids all get bigger, and it is so much fun to see!"

SCRIPTURE SUPPORT: GENESIS 1:27 ESV

So, God created man in his own image, in the image of God he created him; male and female he created them.

Rainbow Reflection: Start Over When Necessary

My sister watched the children while we were out of town. It was Halloween season and let's just say she has a "bit" of a sweet tooth. Since her children are grown, she was delighted with the obscene number of fun-size bars and candy in the house.

After the kids were in bed and the house was quiet, she had a personal Halloween party and enjoyed more candy bars than the "recommended serving."

Thinking she had covered her tracks and discreetly placed the wrappers in the trash, she woke up the next morning to hear Drew calling loud enough for all to hear,

"Holy moly, Aunt Nici, who ate all these candy bars?"

They all had a good laugh and ate more candy because it is Aunt Nici's job to spoil her nieces and nephew.

YOU'RE SPECIAL

SCRIPTURE SUPPORT: 1 CORINTHIANS 9:27 ESV

But I discipline my body and keep it under control,
lest after preaching to others I myself should be disqualified.

Rainbow Reflection:
Find Your Happy Self

Whenever I'm grumpy, it isn't long before Drew reminds me to cheer up using one of his favorite phrases: "Mommy, go find your happy self."

SCRIPTURE SUPPORT: JAMES 1:2-3

Count it all joy, my brothers, when you meet trials of various kinds, for you know that the testing of your faith produces steadfastness.

Rainbow Reflection: Hold Friendships Dear

"I have one song I love to sing, and it says, friends are like flowers in the garden of life. I think that is true," says a friend with Asperger syndrome.

SCRIPTURE SUPPORT: SONG OF SOLOMON 2:12 ESV

The flowers appear on the earth, the time of singing has come, and the voice of the turtledove is heard in our land.

Rainbow Reflection:
Find Joy in Bringing Joy to Others

Doug is exceptional in many ways, but one of the best is his talent for Elvis impersonation.

He says, "My favorite thing about myself is to entertain everyone as Elvis and make them happy."

SCRIPTURE SUPPORT: MATTHEW 22:39 ESV

And a second is like it: You shall love your neighbor as yourself.

Rainbow Reflection:
Take Care of One Another

Friendship is always welcome but individuals with exceptionalities seem to elevate the appreciation of a good friend. It is common to see them greet one another with open arms and laughter. "Friends and family keep you company and help you out."

SCRIPTURE SUPPORT: ECCLESIASTES 4:12 ESV

And though a man might prevail against one who is alone, two will withstand him –
a threefold cord is not quickly broken.

Rainbow Reflection: Understand the Importance of Love

Doug and Debbie are individuals with exceptionalities who have been married for twenty-five years. They are in agreement when they share, "It is important to have someone you are close to and who you love."

SCRIPTURE SUPPORT: JOHN 15:13

Greater love has no one than this, that someone lay down his life for his friends.

Rainbow Reflection:
Trust, Be Open, and Learn

Drew's first communication was through tears. Tears came often and in plenty; he was a colicky baby. After his baptism, the priest joined the family for brunch and as he was leaving, he asked if he could chat with me. He looked me intently in the eye and said, "Some babies are more challenging than others and require an immense amount of patience, but they are all gifts." He went on to say, "I think Drew may come with some challenges, but he will also provide many blessings." I had no idea what he was trying to tell me or how he knew this about Drew, who was only six weeks old. However, he was correct, as Drew has faced many obstacles but has taught us numerous lessons and provided many blessings.

SCRIPTURE SUPPORT: PSALMS 56:3-4 ESV

When I am afraid, I put my trust in you. In God, whose word I praise, in God I trust; I shall not be afraid. What can flesh do to me?

Rainbow Reflection:
Have Courage

John has Williams syndrome but he never shys away from trying new experiences. He pushed himself to join drama club and it was a big success. "I'm most proud of facing my fears such as stage fright. Had I not pushed myself, I would have missed so much fun."

SCRIPTURE SUPPORT: HEBREWS 11:6 ESV

And without faith it is impossible to please him, for whoever would draw near to God must believe that he exists and that he rewards those who seek him.

Rainbow Reflection: Remember That It Is Better to Give Than to Receive

At a birthday party to celebrate a friend with cerebral palsy, the birthday boy commented, "I do like to get presents, but it is also fun to give presents, and God does say that it is better to give than to receive."

SCRIPTURE SUPPORT: MARK 12:31 ESV

"The second is this: 'You shall love your neighbor as yourself.'
There is no other commandment greater than these."

Rainbow Reflection: Remember That It Is All About Love

The notion of love seems to come naturally to so many exceptional children.

I overheard a child with Down syndrome comment, "God says it is most important to love."

I wonder why this simple lesson is so difficult for much of the world to embrace.

SCRIPTURE SUPPORT: COLOSSIANS 3:14 ESV

And above all these put on love,
which binds everything together in perfect harmony.

Rainbow Reflection:
Always Pray

Drew shares, "I was at the University of Dayton Flyers basketball game and Dayton was losing so I said a prayer and asked, 'God, please help the Dayton Flyers make this shot,' and they did! See, he can do anything!"

SCRIPTURE SUPPORT: MATTHEW 21:22 ESV

"And whatever you ask in prayer, you will receive, if you have faith."

Rainbow Reflection:
Enjoy Every Step of the Journey

We could be taking a fabulous vacation and Drew will be most excited about the treats he gets on the plane.

"I love vacation because on the plane rides I get cookies, pop, and peanuts."

SCRIPTURE SUPPORT: ECCLESIASTES 2:24 ESV

There is nothing better for a person than that he should eat and drink and find enjoyment in his toil. This also, I saw, is from the hand of God.

Rainbow Reflection: Hold Angels Close to your Heart

Drew puts faith into action.

He says, "Sometimes when I lose something, I say a prayer to St. Anthony."

"Tony, Tony, look around, something is lost, and it must be found," he continues.

"The saints can take my prayers to Jesus, and he will help me, and guess what, it usually works!" Drew exclaims

SCRIPTURE SUPPORT: JOHN 15:7 ESV

If you abide in me, and my words abide in you,
ask whatever you wish, and it will be done for you.

Rainbow Reflection: Recognize Your Gifts

Why is it that we often focus intently on our developmental areas and hardly recognize our strengths? The opposite seems to be true for individuals with exceptionalities.

"My favorite thing about myself is my laugh; it is funny, and it makes other people laugh."

They seem to recognize and celebrate so much.

SCRIPTURE SUPPORT: PSALMS 126:2 ESV

Then our mouth was filled with laughter, and our tongue with shouts of joy; then they said among the nations, "The Lord has done great things for them."

Rainbow Reflection:
Spend Time with Others

"Someone to be with you is good," Drew so insightfully shares.

SCRIPTURE SUPPORT: HEBREWS 10:25

Not neglecting to meet together, as is the habit of some, but encouraging one another, and all the more as you see the Day drawing near.

Rainbow Reflection:
Invite Conversation

Drew is very social when we are out in the community. In fact, he is invigorated by human interaction and will engage with anyone and everyone. He invites people in so authentically, and the interaction is almost always a blessing. Recently, we were at the grocery when Drew noticed a woman in her eighties wearing a floral dress and said, "You look so pretty in your dress."

She just looked up at him with the biggest smile and said, "It has been a while since a gentleman has paid me such a nice compliment; thank you!"

They enjoyed a pleasant conversation and Drew gave her a "You're Special" rainbow card and in return she gave him a big hug.

That easily, they shifted the momentum of the day. Drew made her smile and she lifted him up in spirit; they both walked away smiling and feeling better.

SCRIPTURE SUPPORT: COLOSSIANS 4:6

Let your speech always be gracious, seasoned with salt, so that you may know how you ought to answer each person.

Rainbow Reflection:
Practice Patience

Drew came home from school and I had prepared snack at the table which included a bagel, some fruit, and a glass of milk. He was home less than five minutes when I heard a crash to discover he had knocked over the entire glass of milk. I got frustrated and he looked at me blankly and stated, "Mommy, you need to be more patient." The irony of getting upset over "spilled milk" was not lost on me.

SCRIPTURE SUPPORT: 1 THESSALONIANS 5:14 ESV

And we urge you, brothers, admonish the idle, encourage the fainthearted, help the weak and be patient with them all.

OCTOBER 7

Rainbow Reflection: Be Childlike

When going out to eat, Drew will bring along his toy animals or football helmets and immediately make friends; sometimes it is with kids, other times adults, but he always connects with people. On one occasion, a grown man in his forties played with Drew for a long time. When he was leaving, I thanked him for being so kind and patient to give Drew so much of his time. He said, "Are you kidding? That is the most fun I've had all week. Do you know how lucky you are to have someone to remind you of your inner child? He is a great kid!"

SCRIPTURE SUPPORT: MATTHEW 19:14 ESV

But Jesus said, "Let the little children come to me and do not hinder them, for to such belongs the kingdom of heaven."

Rainbow Reflection:
See the Special in You

"Everyone is special because God gives everyone talents." Drew goes on to say, "I make rainbows, some people sing, some people are really nice, and you make good food, Mommy!"

SCRIPTURE SUPPORT: 1 CORINTHIANS 12:4

Now there are varieties of gifts, but the same Spirit.

Rainbow Reflection: Have Some Fun Today

Drew reminds me that the best times are spent with others, "I go on dates with Grandma Bev; she takes me to the UD Flyer games and Kentucky Fried Chicken and we have so much fun."

SCRIPTURE SUPPORT: ECCLESIASTES 9:7 ESV

Go, eat your bread with joy, and drink you wine with a merry heart, for God has already approved what you do.

Treasure Time with Those You Love

Drew values time spent together more than anything else. He says, "Mommy, my favorite is when all the family is together; I love to see my grandma and grandpa, my cousins, my aunts and uncles; that is my favorite."

SCRIPTURE SUPPORT: 1 TIMOTHY 1:5 ESV

The aim of our charge is love, that issues from a pure heart
and a good conscience and a sincere faith.

Rainbow Reflection:
Speak the Truth

A strategy I've relied on over the years is the old "Mommy knows best" trick. If I suspected one of the children snuck candy or broke something, I would ask which of the three children was guilty. Of course, I would get three heads shaking side to side, indicating, "no one" had any clue about how this betrayal could have occurred.

As a result, I would ask them to show me their tongues because mothers have the special gift of spotting "fibbers," because their tongue would be jet black! I had a hard time keeping a straight face, but this worked every time, as the guilty party would never stick out their tongue.

Following this discussion, the three would spend the next ten minutes sticking out their tongues, while looking in the mirror with sheer dismay at this special gift I had as a mother.

Fast forward sixteen years, and it still works on Drew. He often says, "It is a bad idea to lie, and you definitely can't lie to Mommy because she will know!"

SCRIPTURE SUPPORT: PROVERBS 12:19 ESV

Truthful lips endure forever, but a lying tongue is but for a moment.

OCTOBER 12

Rainbow Reflection: Understand the Need for Connection

Once a month Drew goes to a gathering for children with exceptionalities. He looks forward to seeing everyone, but he especially cannot wait to see one girl who he has a crush on, and she feels the same way.

Drew and his crush are adorable, kind, and respectful. They talk, hang out, play with toys, and sit beside one another whenever possible.

One visit, they were sitting particularly close to one another, so I casually said, "Let's make some room for Jesus between the two of you."

Drew's friend quickly put me in my place and replied, "Jesus can sit on the other couch, because I want to sit close to my Drew!"

SCRIPTURE SUPPORT: SONG OF SOLOMON 7:6 ESV

How beautiful and pleasant you are, O loved one, with all your delights!

Rainbow Reflection:
Find Common Ground

It is common to overhear or observe individuals with exceptionalities focus on things in common versus bicker over differences.

Drew says, "Mommy, we are all different, but we are all Americans."

SCRIPTURE SUPPORT: COLOSSIANS 4:6 ESV

Let your speech always be gracious, seasoned with salt, so that you may know how you ought to answer each person.

Rainbow Reflection:
Share in Your Abundance

"We should share our food," says one friend with cognition delay as she enjoyed her dinner.

A simple idea that could solve much.

SCRIPTURE SUPPORT: 1 TIMOTHY 6:18 ESV

They are to do good, to be rich in good works, to be generous and ready to share.

Rainbow Reflection: Surprise Others

Whenever we are on road trips, we keep treats and Drew's Rainbow Cards stocked in the car. Drew randomly passes out the goodies and enjoys the surprise and delight in people's reactions. Toll booth workers have provided some of the best responses from the unexpected surprises. When we pull up, Drew hands them some candy and a hand-drawn rainbow in addition to the required toll. You would think they were given a winning lottery ticket!

Some reactions include, "I have never been given anything like this in my booth."

"Oh, I love rainbows; I will keep this right here to make me smile and brighten my day."

Little do they know; their reaction made our day.

SCRIPTURE SUPPORT: 2 PETER 1:7 ESV

And godliness with brotherly affection, and brotherly affection with love.

Rainbow Reflection: Really Try to See People

It particularly tugs at Drew's heart when he sees the homeless. If we are walking downtown, he struggles to walk by anyone homeless. We often bring along bags filled with snack items, gloves, or socks and always his Rainbow Cards to pass out.

On one occasion, I discouraged Drew from sharing his card because the homeless individual was under a big blanket and seemed to be sleeping. For some reason, Drew struggled to keep walking without acknowledging this man.

Before I realized it, Drew ran back and slid his rainbow card and a bag of goodies under the man's blanket without saying a word. He ran back to meet me and after we had walked several yards, we heard a young man's voice calling, "Drew, Drew, thank you so much; this means a lot!"

The young man looked about the same age as Drew and it impacted him greatly that Drew "saw" him.

Drew once again was the teacher and reminded me to step out of my comfort zone to comfort and impact others.

SCRIPTURE SUPPORT: PROVERBS 21:21 ESV

Whoever pursues righteousness and kindness will find life,
righteousness, and honor

OCTOBER 17

Rainbow Reflection: Enjoy the Ride

"I don't care about winning, I just want to have fun." A friend with ADHD reminds me have to fun in the process regardless of the outcome.

SCRIPTURE SUPPORT: ECCLESIASTES 3:13 ESV

Also, that everyone should eat and drink and take pleasure in all his toil—this is God's gift to man.

Rainbow Reflection:
Work Toward Inclusion

Although Drew sees little to no playing time during the football season, his enthusiasm and love of team are ever apparent. "I love being part of the Cougar football team."

SCRIPTURE SUPPORT: ROMANS 1:12 ESV

That is, that we may be mutually encouraged by each other's faith,
both yours and mine.

Rainbow Reflection: Acknowledge the Beauty of Friendships in Your Life

Drew and Maria have been good friends for years. They share a similar aptitude and love of sports. As they have gotten older, they often talk on the phone and because Drew does not like the phone by his ear, he always keeps it on speaker.

As a result, and without trying I overhear their entire conversation. The banter is adorable as they discuss what sports teams are playing and who is going to win, often agreeing to disagree over predictions.

The best is what they say each time they end the call.

"Goodbye Drew, my very best friend."

"Goodbye Maria, my very best friend."

SCRIPTURE SUPPORT: PROVERBS 13:20 ESV

Whoever walks with the wise becomes wise,
but the companion of fools will suffer harm.

Rainbow Reflection:
Be Truthful

"It is a bad idea to lie," a simple reminder from a friend with Down syndrome.

SCRIPTURE SUPPORT: PROVERBS 16:28 ESV

A dishonest man spreads strife, and a whisperer separates close friends.

OCTOBER 21

Rainbow Reflection: Treasure the Moments You Spend with Family and Friends

One day about three weeks after Drew's sister, Alexandra, went off to college, I walked in to find Drew crying quietly in his room. When I came and sat by him, he looked at me with alligator tears and said, "Mommy, I miss Alexandra so much, and I like it best when she is home."

SCRIPTURE SUPPORT: EPHESIANS 4:2 ESV

With all humility and gentleness, with patience, bearing with one another in love.

Rainbow Reflection:
Remember with the Lord, We Live
Forever

"I feel sad when people die, but they get to go to heaven and that makes me happy."

SCRIPTURE SUPPORT: JOHN 6:40 ESV

For this is the will of my Father, that everyone who looks on the Son and believes in him should have eternal life, and I will raise him up on the last day.

Rainbow Reflection:
Listen to Your Body

"I just couldn't keep my eyes open, so my body was telling me it was time to rest."

SCRIPTURE SUPPORT: PSALMS 127:2 ESV

It is in vain that you rise up early and go late to rest, eating the bread of anxious toil; for he gives to his beloved sleep.

Rainbow Reflection:
Find Comfort in the Arts

"Music is my refuge. Music is always there for me when I need it most. It has mended me in so many ways and saved me from feeling like I was a nobody," comments a friend with Williams syndrome.

SCRIPTURE SUPPORT: 1 CORINTHIANS 14:15 ESV

What am I to do? I will pray with my spirit, but I will pray with my mind also; I will sing praise with my spirit, but I will sing with my mind also.

OCTOBER 25

Rainbow Reflection:
Shine Your Best Light

Drew often reminds me of civility, simple kindness, and manners. When he hears "bad language," he often says, "Uh-oh, I heard a bad word. People shouldn't say that; we should say nice things."

SCRIPTURE SUPPORT: EPHESIANS 4:29 ESV

Let no corrupting talk come out of your mouths, but only such as is good for building up, as fits the occasion, that it may give grace to those who hear.

OCTOBER 26

Rainbow Reflection:
Invest Time in Those You Love

"I like to hang out with my sister because I like to enjoy time with her, and she teaches me things."

SCRIPTURE SUPPORT: PSALMS 133:1 ESV

A Song of Ascents. Of David. Behold, how good and pleasant
it is when brothers dwell in unity!

Rainbow Reflection:
Tell Someone You Love Them

It is 6:30 a.m.-ish on any random day,

"Mommy, are you awake?" Silence.

"Mommy, are you awake?" If I ignore him, maybe he will go away.

"Mommy, are you awake?" Now he is tapping on my arm.

"Mommy, are you awake?" He is gently shaking my body.

"My goodness, now I am—what is it, Drew?"

"I love you."

SCRIPTURE SUPPORT: JOHN 13:34-35 ESV

A new commandment I give to you, that you love one another: just as I have loved
you, you also are to love one another. By this all people will know that you are my
disciples, if you have love for one another.

Rainbow Reflection:
Be Thoughtful

"You should always treat people with respect; that is what Grandfather says."

SCRIPTURE SUPPORT: 1 PETER 2:17 ESV

Honor everyone. Love the brotherhood. Fear God. Honor the emperor.

Rainbow Reflection:
Acknowledge Beauty in ALL His Works

It is inspiring how individuals with exceptionalities see the beauty in most everything.

Drew calls loudly as he looks out the window, "Hurry, hurry…it is snowing, look how beautiful!"

SCRIPTURE SUPPORT: ISAIAH 55:10 ESV

For as the rain and the snow come down from heaven and do not return there but water the earth, making it bring forth and sprout, giving seed to the sower and bread to the eater.

Rainbow Reflection:
Hug Someone Every Day

After getting a hug from Gapper, the Cincinnati Reds mascot, Drew says, "A hug is a way to show love, and the funny thing is I feel good when I get a hug, but I feel even better when I give a hug."

SCRIPTURE SUPPORT: JOHN 13 34-35 ESV

"A new commandment I give to you, that you love one another; just as I have loved you, you also are to love one another. By this all people will know that you are my disciples, if you have lover for one another."

OCTOBER 31

Rainbow Reflection: Pray for Others Even When It Is Hard

While watching the news, Drew is often moved to prayer. If he hears a story about someone who has committed a crime, I am often surprised how Drew remembers to pray for the criminal as well as the victim.

"He shouldn't do those things, but I will pray for him."

SCRIPTURE SUPPORT: MATTHEW 5:44 ESV

But I say to you, love your enemies and pray for those who persecute you.

Rainbow Reflection:
Keep Family and Friends Close

"When our whole family is together, I feel safe."

SCRIPTURE SUPPORT: 1 JOHN 3:11 ESV

For this is the message that you have heard from the beginning,
that we should love one another.

Rainbow Reflection: Be Trusting and Optimistic

Drew has unwavering faith in God's forgiveness and everlasting life. Recently driving past a very large cemetery he looked at the rows of headstones and stared in amazement.

I was concerned and said, "I know that cemeteries can be a little scary and overwhelming, buddy."

Smiling as he looked out at all the headstones he replied, "No, Mommy, just look at all of those people in heaven."

I drove quietly on in disbelief at how he views the world and how his perspective so often invites peace and comfort.

SCRIPTURE SUPPORT: JOSHUA 1:9 ESV

Have I not commanded you? Be strong and courageous, do not be frightened, and do not be dismayed, for the Lord your God is with you wherever you go.

Rainbow Reflection:
Look Out for One Another

After leaving Drew's 12th birthday party, his cousin Christian came away with a deeper understanding of Drew's potential limitations. Up to this time they parallel played with much delight, but as years passed and the gap grew, the deficits were more obvious.

On the drive home, Christian was processing what he had noticed and expressed concern to his mother. "How will Drew take care of himself if something happens to Aunt Kathy and Uncle Dave?"

His mother was considering the best response to reassure her son but before she could articulate an answer, Christian said with 100% confidence, "Never mind, Mom; I'll just take care of him."

SCRIPTURE SUPPORT: 1 JOHN 3:17 ESV

But if anyone has the world's good and sees his brother in need, yet closes his heart against him, how does God's love abide in him.

Rainbow Reflection: Love with All You Have

A s we are hugging, Drew says, "Thank you, Jesus, for my mommy."

I reflect that I am the *lucky* one to be blessed with Drew, a beautiful and precious gift from God.

SCRIPTURE SUPPORT: GALATIANS 3:28 ESV

There is neither Jew nor Greek, there is neither slave nor free,
there is no male and female, for you are all one in Christ Jesus.

Rainbow Reflection:
Speak with Positive Intentions

"Grandma Bev says to accentuate the positive and to encourage others, and Grandpa Ron says everything will work out, and I think they are both right," Drew exclaims.

SCRIPTURE SUPPORT: MARK 11:24 ESV

Therefore, I tell you, whatever you ask in prayer,
believe that you have received it, and it will be yours.

Rainbow Reflection:
Give the Gift of Time

It doesn't take too much time to play with Drew, and a quick hand of cards or a matchbox car race bring him so much joy.

"Thank you for playing with me."

SCRIPTURE SUPPORT: JAMES 4:14 ESV

Yet you do not know what tomorrow will bring. What is your life?
For you are a mist that appears for a little time and then vanishes.

Rainbow Reflection:
Recognize the Little Things
That Spark Joy

It doesn't take much to spark joy for most individuals with exceptionalities.

One day I asked Drew, "If you could have anything in the world today, what would it be?"

It made me laugh when he replied, "I would get three cheese coneys and a cold pop."

SCRIPTURE SUPPORT: PSALMS 30:12

That my glory may sing your praise and not be silent.
O LORD my God, I will give thanks to you forever!

Rainbow Reflection:
Show Support for Someone Today

Drew has a loving community that surrounds him, but he never takes it for granted.

He says, "I never give up, because so many people cheer for me."

SCRIPTURE SUPPORT: 1 JOHN 4:19-21 ESV

We love because he first loved us. If anyone says, "I love God," and hates his brother, he is a liar; for he who does not love his brother whom he has seen cannot love God whom he has not seen. And this commandment we have from him; whoever loves God must also love his brother.

Rainbow Reflection: Remember That God Gave You Everything You Need to Succeed

"**M**ommy, why are you so sad?"

"I'm not sad, Drew, I just have a big project and a challenging process, and I'm a bit stressed."

"Mommy, you are enough."

SCRIPTURE SUPPORT: MATTHEW 5:14 ESV

You are the light of the world. A city set on a hill cannot be hidden.

Rainbow Reflection:
Push Your Comfort Level

As a result of sensory issues, Drew would never put his face in water. For years we worked with swim instructors, therapists, and as a family to help him overcome this barrier but with no success.

While on a family vacation, we went snorkeling and swimming in the ocean. Drew was my partner but simply held onto my hand with his head above water. He began to overhear excited snorkelers come up from the water to exclaim they had seen a sea turtle, clown fish, or some other fascinating creature.

Drew, who loves any type of animal, couldn't stand it any longer and simply began snorkeling. His desire to explore overshadowed his fear.

Back on the boat he excitedly told anyone who would listen, "I did it; I put my face in the water. I heard everyone talking about all the fish under the water, so I wanted to see for myself. I was scared, but I did it!"

SCRIPTURE SUPPORT: PSALMS 56: 3-4

When I am afraid, I put my trust in you. In God, whose word I praise, in God I trust; I shall not be afraid. What can flesh do to me?

Rainbow Reflection: Serve Others Daily

Numerous times on any given day, the family and others help Drew, but he has also learned to serve.

Without fail and multiple times per day, I can count on Drew to ask, "Mommy, can I help you?"

SCRIPTURE SUPPORT: ECCLESIASTES 4:9-10 ESV

Two are better than one, because they have a good reward for their toil. For if they fall, one will lift up his fellow. But woe to him who is alone when he falls and has not another to lift him up.

Rainbow Reflection:
Initiate Conversations

Drew was waiting his turn for a haircut and started chatting with an older woman. I was somewhat concerned because she looked frustrated, and I didn't want him to bother her.

However, during the conversation, I noticed she became more relaxed and jovial. When they called her name for her haircut, she asked them to wait as she walked over to me and through tears explained, "I was married fifty-two years and my husband recently died and my family lives out of town. Lately, I have been so sad and lonely. The conversation I just had with your son was the best thing that has happened to me in a very long time. Can I hug your son?"

SCRIPTURE SUPPORT: 1 TIMOTHY 5:17-18

Let the elders who rule well be considered worthy of double honor, especially those who labor in preaching and teaching. For the Scripture says, "You shall not muzzle an ox when it treads out the grain," and "The laborer deserves his wages."

Rainbow Reflection: Do What Makes You Happy

Individuals with exceptionalities seem to do what brings them joy despite their level of talent.

Our friend with cognition delay proclaims, "Singing makes me happy, so I like to do it a lot."

SCRIPTURE SUPPORT: JAMES 5:13

Is anyone among you suffering? Let him pray. Is anyone cheerful?
Let him sing praise.

Rainbow Reflection: Avoid Worry

When Drew was turning sixteen, we suspected that driving might not be in his future, but being a milestone birthday, we wanted to throw a surprise celebration. Drew doesn't have any "best friends" or even friends that he regularly hangs out with, but Drew is friends with everyone.

He also has connection with a large group of young men that he played Cougar football with from the 3rd-5th grade, but five years had passed since that time. I decided that with an extended group of kids and our family, there would be enough of a group to make a celebration, so we planned a surprise 16th party.

The day of Drew's birthday arrived, and we were ready. The balloons were flying, the birthday banner was up, and the rainbow cake was waiting! Everything was in place except for my nerves.

Two hours before the party, I couldn't quiet the voice in my head that was questioning,

What were you thinking? No one is going to show. Why would these high school boys come to Drew's birthday party?

But I was so wrong! One by one, the guests arrived. They showed up with smiles, high fives, gifts, and authentic hugs. By the time Drew arrived for his surprise, over eighty people had come to celebrate his big day.

Drew was elated to see all his "best friends."

At the end of the party I went up to one buddy, Jack, and said, "Thanks to you and all the boys for coming to Drew's party; it means so much to him and to our family."

Jack looked at me, a bit confused, and said, "Mrs. Leurck, we wouldn't have missed this for the world. We love seeing Drew; he is our friend."

SCRIPTURE SUPPORT: MATTHEW 6:27 ESV

And which of you by being anxious can add a single hour to his span of life.

NOVEMBER 15

Rainbow Reflection: Violence Is Never Right but God's Mercy Is Greater

"Everyone should go to heaven, but people that kill others should ask God to forgive them." Drew seems to understand that if we ask God for forgiveness, it will be granted.

SCRIPTURE SUPPORT: PROVERBS 3:31 ESV

Do not envy a man of violence and do not choose any of his ways.

Rainbow Reflection: Friendship Endures and You May Never Know the Impact

Cameron was Drew's friend in grade school. They waited for the bus together, they jumped on the trampoline together, they played football. They were buddies.

As boys grow and mature, naturally so do their interests. This is where the disconnect happens; Drew's buddies move on while Drew is stuck at age seven. When other boys are driving cars and selecting colleges, Drew still wants to play Star Wars, animals, and matchbox cars.

Cameron, however, made time for Drew and always showed kindness and love. Eventually Cameron and his family moved, and he went to a different high school, so he and Drew rarely saw one another. Many high school boys would forget about a special friend from grade school, but not Cameron.

He heard about a Drew's Rainbows Foundation event at Dewey's Pizza and insisted to his mother that they attend. So much time had passed that she was surprised her son was so interested in attending, but she happily agreed to go.

When Cameron walked into the restaurant and Drew saw his friend, Drew jumped for joy, hugged him, and said, "Mommy, can you believe it? My old buddy Cameron is here."

They interacted like no time had passed and Cameron left with a rainbow card, a full belly of pizza, and a happy heart.

Several years passed; Cameron went to college and Drew was busy in his job training program when one evening we got a phone call about a terrible accident. Drew's good buddy Cameron had devastatingly been fatally injured.

Almost eighteen months following Cameron's death, I got a message from his mother. She was cleaning out Cameron's wallet to find Drew's Rainbow Card. Her message to me read,

"I was going through Cam's wallet and found Drew's rainbow card. The card must have meant a lot to Cam, because his wallet was perfectly organized with only the necessary things in it including Drew's card."

The treasure of friendship.

SCRIPTURE SUPPORT: ROMANS 12:9 ESV

Let love be genuine. Abhor what is evil; hold fast to what is good.

Rainbow Reflection:
Gratitude

Drew's prayers are simple but always so meaningful.

"Dear Jesus, please help the people who don't have a warm home tonight, and thank you very much for mine."

SCRIPTURE SUPPORT: PSALMS 136:1 ESV

Give thanks to the Lord, for he is good, for his steadfast love endures forever.

Rainbow Reflection:
Be Generous Even When It Is Hard

"When I have to share ice cream, I feel a bit fussy; I wish I could keep it all to myself, but I know I should share." Drew understands the importance of giving.

SCRIPTURE SUPPORT: PROVERBS 11:24 ESV

One gives freely, yet grows all the richer, another withholds what he should give, and only suffers want. Whoever brings blessing will be enriched, and one who waters will himself be watered.

Rainbow Reflection:
Find Encouragement in Everlasting Life

Drew's great-aunt and uncle suffered unimaginable loss when two of their sons passed within two years of one another. The extended family went to mass to celebrate Aunt Kathy and Uncle Steve's anniversary and Drew was seated next to Aunt Kathy. Without cause or warning, Drew quietly took Aunt Kathy's hand and whispered to her, "It is okay, Aunt Kathy; Matt and Paul are in heaven."

She later told me she had no idea of how Drew knew she was struggling during mass, but his words of encouragement provided strength and comfort.

SCRIPTURE SUPPORT: JOHN 10:9

I am the door. If anyone enters by me, he will be saved
and will go in and out and find pasture.

Rainbow Reflection: Watch Over Each Other

"**M**ommy, don't worry. I will watch over my sisters when I grow up." Drew has an instinctual need for caregiving; it comes so naturally to him.

SCRIPTURE SUPPORT: 1 TIMOTHY 5:8 ESV

But if anyone does not provide for his relatives, and especially for members of his household, he has denied the faith.

Rainbow Reflection:
Share Your Love and Your Life

"Genevieve, you are such a good puppy; I'm so glad we got you in our family."

SCRIPTURE SUPPORT: GENESIS 1:21 ESV

So, God created the great sea creatures and every living creature that moves, with which the waters swarm, according to their kinds, and every winged bird according to its kind. And God saw that it was good.

Rainbow Reflection: Respond with Love

Watching the news can be difficult for Drew as he cannot comprehend why people act violently. "Mommy, why do people do bad things and hurt one another? Don't they know that they are supposed to love one another?"

SCRIPTURE SUPPORT: 1 CORINTHIANS 13:4-8 ESV

Love is patient and kind, love does not envy or boast, it is not arrogant or rude. It does not insist on its own way, it is not irritable or resentful; it does not rejoice at wrongdoing but rejoices with the truth. Love bears all things, believes all things, hopes all things, endures all things. Love never ends. As for prophecies, they will pass away; as for tongues, they will cease, as for knowledge, it will pass away.

Rainbow Reflection:
Honor Your Parents

Drew is very generous with his hugs and his words. Multiple times a day, we are lucky to hear him say, "I love you, Mommy and Daddy."

SCRIPTURE SUPPORT: EXODUS 20:12 ESV

"Honor your father and your mother, that your days may be long in the land that the Lord your god is giving you."

Rainbow Reflection: Pray & Trust

"St. Michael watches over and protects me; he will watch over you, too; all you have to do is ask." Drew's comment demonstrates his ever-present faith.

SCRIPTURE SUPPORT: PSALMS 91:11 ESV

For he will command his angels concerning you to guard you in all your ways.

Rainbow Reflection: Recognize Everyone and the Gifts They Have to Offer

"When I am part of the team, people only see me and what I can do. They don't see my Williams syndrome."

SCRIPTURE SUPPORT: LUKE 6:37 ESV

"Judge not, and you will not be judged; condemn not, and you will not be condemned; forgive, and you will be forgiven."

NOVEMBER 26

Rainbow Reflection: Do the Right Thing

"God says that it is not good to lie, and besides, Santa would know!"

SCRIPTURE SUPPORT: JOHN 14:15

If you love me, you will keep my commandments.

Rainbow Reflection:
Receive Graciously

Drew understands the importance of gratitude and manners. He says, "I can't wait for my birthday and I love opening my presents, but I know that I have to say thank you!"

SCRIPTURE SUPPORT: JAMES 1:17 ESV

Every good gift and every perfect gift is from above, coming down from the Father of lights with whom there is no variation or shadow due to change.

Rainbow Reflection:
Keep Hope Alive

"The Reds are on a really long losing streak, but I just know they will win again; I believe in them, and you can never give up!"

SCRIPTURE SUPPORT: PSALMS 71:14 ESV

But I hope continually and will praise you yet more and more.

Rainbow Reflection: Pray for Strength

When schedules change, Drew will ask, repeatedly and often, what is happening next. He already knows the answer to his questions, but he yearns for reassurance and order.

"Mommy, when is the school break over? Mommy, when is the school break over? Mommy, when is the school break over?"

Part of Drew's order in life is a set schedule, knowing what is happening next and a reliable schedule makes him at ease. He gets very anxious when things are out of sync and will "spin." This is not literal, but rather talking in circles and asking repeatedly about the schedule. He struggles with anxiety and together we often pray for help while striving to remain calm and at peace.

SCRIPTURE SUPPORT: 1 PETER 5:6-7 ESV

Humble yourselves, therefore, under the mighty hand of God so that at the proper time he may exalt you, casting all your anxieties on him, because he cares for you.

Rainbow Reflection:
Recognize the Glory of God Within You

"Disabilities is just a word and I do not let it define me. Either you let it define you or you define yourself." John defines himself and he is exceptional.

SCRIPTURE SUPPORT: JOHN 9:1-3 ESV

As he passed by, he saw a man blind from birth. And his disciples asked him, "Rabbi, who sinned, this man or his parents, that he was born blind?" Jesus answered, "It was not that this man sinned, or his parents, but that the works of God might be displayed in him."

Rainbow Reflection:
Show Joy and Allow It to Be Contagious

At age twenty-two, Drew still jumps up and down when he sees Santa at Macy's department store. People in line often get very touched and even emotional as they observe his exuberance. It is as if Drew enables their inner child to be released and to remember such Christmas joy.

SCRIPTURE SUPPORT: ISAIAH 55:12 ESV

For you shall go out in joy and be led forth in peace; the mountains and the hills before you shall break forth into singing, and all the trees of the field shall clap their hands.

Rainbow Reflection:
Family Comes in Many Forms

Deb is a dear friend and has played an important role in Drew's life.

He says, "Some people are family even though we aren't related, like Ms. Deb."

SCRIPTURE SUPPORT: PROVERBS 27:10 ESV

Do not forsake your friend and your father's friend, and do not go to your brother's house in the day of your calamity. Better is a neighbor who is near than a brother who is far away.

Rainbow Reflection:
Make Time for Play Time

Ryan and Drew are first cousins who are both exceptional in their own way. They can play for hours and find comfort and peace in one another's company. Often with very few words exchanged, they seem to understand on a level that most cannot achieve with the use of many words.

"Ryan and I have fun together; we play helmets and animals."

SCRIPTURE SUPPORT: PROVERBS 27:19 ESV

As in water face reflects face, so the heart of man reflects man

DECEMBER 4

Rainbow Reflection: Honesty Is the Best Policy

Drew cannot keep a secret, as he inherently feels he is being dishonest. One Christmas he went shopping with his father and they had several conversations about keeping the gifts a secret until Christmas morning. Drew seemed to understand but upon returning home from shopping he immediately came in the door calling,

"Mommy, Daddy bought you a necklace for Christmas."

SCRIPTURE SUPPORT: LUKE 12:2

Nothing is covered up that will not be revealed or hidden that will not be known.

Rainbow Reflection:
Compliment Others

Drew knows how to make people smile and is quick to share compliments. He says,

"I like your food Grandma."

SCRIPTURE SUPPORT: ROMANS 15:2 ESV

Let each of us please his neighbor for his good, to build him up.

DECEMBER 6

Rainbow Reflection: Never Underestimate How Important We Are to One Another

For many years, we have visited the same Santa at Macy's. He is very special and always so kind to our family. In 2016, Santa heard about Drew and his rainbows and found a rainbow angel ornament to give to Drew as a Christmas gift.

Each day when Santa went to Macy's, he faithfully brought the gift, unsure of when Drew would visit. December 22nd arrived, and when our family still had not visited, Santa was concerned that perhaps this was the year that Drew, at age eighteen, no longer believed.

The next day, as our family walked into the department store, Santa spotted us. He was so happy that he asked the children in line to wait as he got up, walked over to Drew, and gave him a big hug. Of course, Drew still believed and was jumping up and down yelling, "Santa!"

No one in line was angered, as it was apparent that Santa and Drew were dear friends. Following the hug, we took our place in line and waited to sit on Santa's lap and Santa was finally able to present his special rainbow ornament.

Years pass and we visit Santa each Christmas, and Drew still believes in Santa with his whole heart. However, 2019 is different. I received an email "From Santa" and I assumed it was spam, but something nagged me to open the message,

Dear Drew,

I have a new home about an hour away from downtown Cincinnati. I know it is far, but I sure hope to see you. Christmas just won't be Christmas if you don't visit.

Love, Santa

We were so touched that the magic Santa had brought to our family for so many years was also important to him. Of course, we made the hour trip, and it was well worth it.

SCRIPTURE SUPPORT: PROVERBS 27:9 ESV

Oil and perfume make the heart glad, and the sweetness of a friend comes from his earnest counsel.

Rainbow Reflection:
Remember That Love Is Universal

Travel is a family passion. Whenever we can, and probably on occasions when we shouldn't, we go. Our travels have included many of the beautiful United States as well as abroad. One thing is consistent: no matter where we go, Drew makes friends.

Drew only speaks English, but through his rainbows he has had conversations with folks who speak French, Italian, Spanish, Hindi, and even Arabic. After a short conversation with an Italian who spoke limited English Drew commented, "Mommy, I didn't really know what he was saying, but when I gave him my rainbow, he smiled, and I knew we were friends."

SCRIPTURE SUPPORT: 1 JOHN 4:16 ESV

So, we have come to know and to believe the love that God has for us. God is love,
and whoever abides in love abides in God, and God abides in him.

MARK 16:15 ESV

And he said to them, "Go into all the world and proclaim
the gospel to the whole creation."

Rainbow Reflection:
Wish Big

We always get a kick out of Drew's wish list at Christmas. It is usually the same and includes very basic and simple requests. Two things that always make the list are reams of paper and markers, so he is abundantly stocked to make his rainbows. As the holiday draws near, I often overhear Drew contemplating, "I'm not sure if I will get them, but I really hope that Santa brings me some paper and markers."

It always warms my heart how simply he is pleased.

SCRIPTURE SUPPORT: HEBREWS 11:1 ESV

Now faith is the assurance of things hoped for, the conviction of things not seen.

Rainbow Reflection:
Be a Positive Example

Drew is always watching and learning from adults around him. On a family outing to dinner, it was touching when Drew handed me his arm saying, "Here, Mommy, I want to give you my arm and open your door like Daddy does."

SCRIPTURE SUPPORT: 1 PETER 5:3 ESV

Not domineering over those in your charge but being examples to the flock.

DECEMBER 10

Rainbow Reflection:
Find Your Happy Place

"I like painting and listening to music because I feel creative and I have time to myself," shares a friend with autism.

SCRIPTURE SUPPORT: MARK 6:31 ESV

And he said to them, "Come away by yourselves to a desolate place and rest awhile. For many were coming and going and they had n leisure even to eat."

Rainbow Reflection: Try Not to Turn a Blind Eye

Drew finds it nearly impossible to ignore someone who is reaching out for help. He never questions motives but is quick to ask, "Hurry up, Mommy, there is a man beside the road asking for help. How can we help him?"

SCRIPTURE SUPPORT: PROVERBS 11:24-25 ESV

One gives freely yet grows all the richer; another withholds what he should give, and only suffers want. Whoever brings blessing will be enriched, and one who waters will himself be watered.

Rainbow Reflection:
Take Chances

A friend of Drew's with Williams syndrome gives the best advice and is always so positive.

"Go for it; take it because it is yours. Your time is now. Being nervous is normal, but break that barrier, because once you do, you cannot be denied or stopped."

SCRIPTURE SUPPORT: 2 CHRONICLES 15:7 ESV

"But you, take courage! Do not let your hands be weak,
for your work shall be rewarded."

Rainbow Reflection:
Be Grateful and Empathetic

"It is so cold today, and some people don't even have a coat. Dear Lord, please help the people who are cold."

SCRIPTURE SUPPORT: EPHESIANS 1:16 ESV

I do not cease to give thanks for you, remembering you in my prayers.

DECEMBER 14

Rainbow Reflection:
Be Generous and Show Compassion

"If I see someone who is sad, I just tell them, it's okay. Sometimes I just sit by them and be quiet and sometimes I give them a hug."

SCRIPTURE SUPPORT: GALATIANS 6:10 ESV

So then, as we have opportunity, let us do good to everyone, and especially to those who are of the household of faith.

Rainbow Reflection: Look Forward with Anticipation

Every May, Drew and his father go to the Kentucky Derby Festivities. Other than Christmas, it is Drew's favorite day of the year. Generally, in April, the countdown begins:

"Dad, it is almost our day; only forty-four days until the Kentucky Derby."

"Dad, it is almost our day; only forty-three days until the Kentucky Derby."

"Dad, it is almost our day; only forty-two days until the Kentucky Derby."

SCRIPTURE SUPPORT: ISAIAH 40:31 ESV

But they who wait for the Lord shall renew their strength; they shall mount up with wings like eagles; they shall run and not be weary; they shall walk and not faint.

Rainbow Reflection: Peace

A never-ending prayer from Drew, "Dear Jesus, please help people to stop fighting."

SCRIPTURE SUPPORT: PHILIPPIANS 4:7

And the peace of God, which surpasses all understanding, will guard your hearts and your minds in Christ Jesus.

Rainbow Reflection:
Know That We Are All Precious Gifts of God with Purpose and Potential

"I think God made us for different purposes and to be here for a reason," says a friend with Asperger syndrome.

SCRIPTURE SUPPORT: ISAIAH 43:8 ESV

Bring out the people who are blind, yet have eyes, who are deaf, yet have ears!

Rainbow Reflection: Self Soothe

Drew strongly prefers solid routines, and even small changes in routine require reassurance. When needed, we review schedule changes or explain disruptions to daily life. The busy holiday season often involves more evenings out, and as Dave and I were preparing to leave, I overheard Drew in his room.

"It is good for Mommy and Daddy to have a date night and they will be home real soon. It will be okay and when they get home, Mommy will kiss me good night."

He repeated this several times, and I realized he was reassuring himself.

SCRIPTURE SUPPORT: 2 THESSALONIANS 3:16

Now may the Lord of peace himself give you peace at all times in every way. The Lord be with you all.

Rainbow Reflection:
See the Signs

At age sixteen, Drew was invited to share his rainbow story to a lecture hall of over 100 students at Miami University. I was worried that it was too much pressure for Drew and uncertain how he would be received by the students. Drew, however, was excited to meet all the students and wanted to participate, so we supported him.

It is an hour to Miami and many concerns were running through my mind and to add to the anxiety, we were driving in thunderstorms the entire way.

Drew, with the wonderful support of my husband, Dave, spoke for a short time and then we shared the Drew Gets It documentary followed by a question and answer session. The presentation was a big success, and the students were engaged and supportive.

One student came up to Drew following the presentation and commented that Drew had given her a lot to think about regarding faith and rainbows representing God's love. They finished their short conversation and since the rain finally stopped, we all walked out of the lecture hall together. To our amazement, we were met with the most spectacular double rainbow we have ever seen.

The student was speechless until she said, "This is just too much!"

Drew simply and innocently replied, "See, I told you—God's love."

SCRIPTURE SUPPORT: 1 JOHN 3:1 ESV

See what kind of love the Father has given to us, that we should be called children of God; and so, we are. The reason why the world does not know us is that it did not know him.

Rainbow Reflection:
Elevate Language

When Drew gets angry, he has a litany of expressions. "Fiddlesticks, rats, son of a nutcracker," are favorites. He explains, "I don't think is a good idea to say bad words, but a lot of people say them."

SCRIPTURE SUPPORT: MATTHEW 15:11 ESV

It is not what goes into the mouth that defiles a person, but what comes out of the mouth; this defiles a person.

Rainbow Reflection:
See Beauty

"Girls are so pretty; they remind me of flowers."

SCRIPTURE SUPPORT: ESV

I praise you, for I am fearfully and wonderfully made.
Wonderful are your works; my soul knows it very well.

Rainbow Reflection:
Just Ask God

"I pray for people to stop fighting, but sometimes I might pray for something I want. Like I might pray to get my markers or to go on a trip someday to see the animals in Africa. I don't think God minds if I ask for things."

SCRIPTURE SUPPORT: MARK 11:24 ESV

Therefore, I tell you, whatever you ask in prayer,
believe that you have received it, and it will be yours.

Rainbow Reflection: Count Your Blessings

Drew doesn't ask for much, nor does he take things for granted.

"Look at everything we have, Mommy; a warm house and all of this food. Dear Jesus, please help the homeless tonight who don't have any food or warm clothes."

SCRIPTURE SUPPORT: HEBREWS 13:5 ESV

Keep your life free from love of money, and be content with what you have, for he has said, "I will never leave you nor forsake you."

Rainbow Reflection: Be Generous

The year after Santa gave Drew the angel ornament, Drew presented Santa with a painting he and his sister had created. "When I gave Santa a present, I was so excited. Santa always gives others presents, so it felt so nice to give him one."

SCRIPTURE SUPPORT: JAMES 1:17 ESV

Every good gift and every perfect gift are from above, coming down from the Father of lights with whom there is no variation or shadow due to change.

Rainbow Reflection:
Give thanks to the Lord Our God

A favorite Christmas prayer Drew shared that says so much with so few words.

"Thank you, Jesus, for being born today, and thank you, Mary, for being a good mommy."

SCRIPTURE SUPPORT: MATTHEW 2:11 ESV

And going into the house they saw the child with Mary his mother, and they fell down and worshiped him. Then, opening their treasures, they offered him gifts, gold and frankincense and myrrh.

DECEMBER 26

Rainbow Reflection: Be Silly Once in A While

"Dad acts like a child and likes to have fun."

SCRIPTURE SUPPORT: LUKE 18:17 ESV

Truly, I say to you, whoever does not receive the kingdom of
God like a child shall not enter it.

Rainbow Reflection:
Cherish Time

Drew always reminds me of the importance of time especially precious time spent with friends and family.

"Mommy, why do we all have to grow up? I wish our family could all just live together forever."

SCRIPTURE SUPPORT: ROMANS 16:16

Greet one another with a holy kiss. All the churches of Christ greet you.

Rainbow Reflection: Talk to God

" I told Uncle Greg that I was talking to Jesus, and he said I can talk to Jesus whenever I want because Jesus is always in my heart."

SCRIPTURE SUPPORT: 1 TIMOTHY 2:8 ESV

I desire then that in every place the men should pray,
lifting holy hands without anger or quarreling.

Rainbow Reflection: Show Affection

The day we wrapped our home with Drew's Rainbows, people came from all over the tri-state area. One family came from Indiana and had a young boy who couldn't wait to meet Drew. Upon seeing Drew for the first time, the little boy jumped into arms with a big hug and shouted, "I just love your rainbows!"

SCRIPTURE SUPPORT: EPHESIANS 4:1-6

I therefore, a prisoner for the Lord, urge you to walk in a manner worthy of the calling to which you have been called, with all humility and gentleness, with patience, bearing with one another in love, eager to maintain the unity of the Spirit in the bond of peace.

DECEMBER 30

Rainbow Reflection:
Share Your Gifts and Talents

We are seated in Cincinnati's Music Hall near the front for a New Year's Eve Symphony Pops concert and the house is full of approximately 1300 in attendance. The headliner sings wonderfully and in between sets, he includes some friendly conversation with the audience:

"Let's hear some of your New Year's Resolutions."

Several audience members comment that they are going to lose weight or exercise, to which the performer jokingly responds:

"Yes, those always make the list."

About that time, Drew loudly calls out, "I want to pass out a rainbow to everyone I meet."

The performer stops in his tracks and asks, "What did you say?"

To which Drew repeats, "I want to pass out a rainbow to everyone I meet."

"What do you mean?" asks the singer.

Drew explains that he thinks that everyone is special, and he likes to pass out rainbows to everyone he meets to remind them just how special they are.

The headliner says, "Young man, you win! That just might be the best resolution I've ever heard."

One rainbow at a time, Drew is determined to remind the world that everyone is special!

SCRIPTURE SUPPORT: HEBREWS 13:16

Do not neglect to do good and to share what you have,
for such sacrifices are pleasing to God.

DECEMBER 31

Rainbow Reflection:
Be Passionate About Your Passion

I can count on Drew to shine his light, share his love, and illuminate life with his beautiful rainbows.

One day as Drew was drawing, I overheard him say, "I don't know why people like my rainbows, but I think I'll just keep making them."

Thanks be to God!

SCRIPTURE SUPPORT: GENESIS 9:13 ESV

I have set my bow in the cloud, and it shall be a sign of the
covenant between me and the earth.

Appendix:

I've learned to never underestimate anyone and that individuals with exceptionalities can do so much to participate in society. Drew has and continues to lead with exceptional accomplishments:

- 2005: Drew's Rainbow "You're Special" Daily Art Begins

- 2005-Current: Drew has passed out more than 20,000 rainbows across the country and internationally

- 2015: Drew's home became his canvas to share his message of love

- 2016: Drew's Rainbows Foundation is founded to recognize & support individuals with exceptionalities

- 2016: The documentary premiere of Drew Gets It is shown to a sold-out crowd of over 500

- 2017: Drew Gets It is selected to be shown in three film festivals

- 2019: Andrew receives the Lovis Foundation Award:

  This award honors students who are going above and beyond to create a positive culture in their schools and communities.

- 2020: DrewsRainbowsArt.com Website created to represent artists with exceptionalities

- 2020: Drew's Rainbow Foundation becomes a Best Buddies Citizens Chapter to support adults with exceptionalities

- 2021: Andrew is selected and honored with Cincinnati Heroes of Character Award

  These Heroes have been nominated by their peers as upstanding citizens and people of character, and represent the best of the Tri-State area. They come from all over the region, from different backgrounds and walks of life. They are willing to do the right thing, no matter who is watching. They set an example of care and compassion in our communities. They may never have met before this event, but they are connected, nonetheless — by their character.

- 2021: Drew's Rainbows Facebook Group created with over 1200 members to inspire others with color and light during the dark pandemic

- 2022: Book Release of You're Special, written by Mom, inspired by individuals with exceptionalities and specifically Drew

Photo Credits:

L to L Photography

Rachel Ruttle Photography

Copy House Films

Drew's Rainbows Group

Debra Shepard Photography

Lourdes Leurck

The Leurck Family

CPSIA information can be obtained
at www.ICGtesting.com
Printed in the USA
BVHW060857221222
654829BV00021B/440